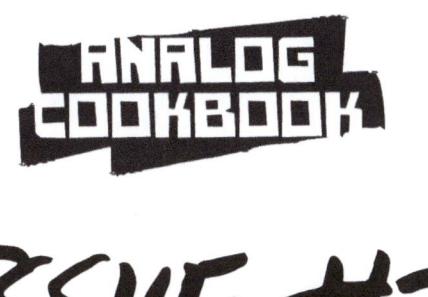

ISSUE #3

Founder/Editor-in-Chief: Kate E. Hinshaw

Photography Editor: Andi Avery

Cover & Interior Design: Katie Greene

Analog Cookbook Logo: Sarah Lawrence's Design Emporium

Questions: hello@analogcookbook.com

Published by Analog Cookbook © 2020

Funded in part by the Beverly Sears Graduate Student Award

With generous support by University of Colorado-Boulder:

Department of Cinema Studies & Moving Image Arts

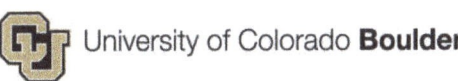

LETTER FROM THE EDITOR

"Don't get into scotch or photography, you can't afford either."

This is what my grandfather used to say. A child of Czechoslovakian immigrants he was fiercely pragmatic and believed that hard work paid off. It worked out for him for him at least.

This pandemic has left us all questioning what we can afford on every level. Many of us get into DIY analog filmmaking because that thrift store 35mm or Super 8mm camera was more affordable than a RED. We process film in bathtubs and fill our tanks with household chemicals because it's less toxic, readily available, and a lot cheaper. Many of our practices were already homebound before COVID.

This year I moved my chemicals out of a darkroom and into a bathroom where I process Ektachrome and hang my film to dry on a clothes rack. Despite its convenience, it has felt terribly difficult to process much of anything these days, let alone a roll of film. With all the tips and tricks we have to make filmmaking cheap and fun and accessible, I find myself questioning if now is the time to be making art. Other days, it just makes sense. Painting film allows me space to process trauma. Scratching film feels good. Seeing film process in front of my eyes allows for a kind of cathartic high that is pure magic.

All that said, there is nothing easy here. It is totally okay to step back from your art practice. After all, rest is a revolutionary act in and of itself. But if messing around with a roll of film feels good, allows you time yourself, and helps you process the world around you, can you really afford not to do it?

– Kate E. Hinshaw

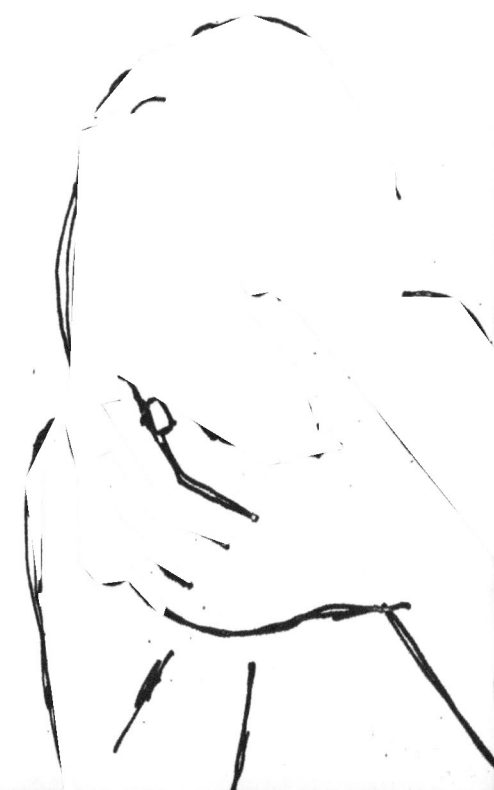

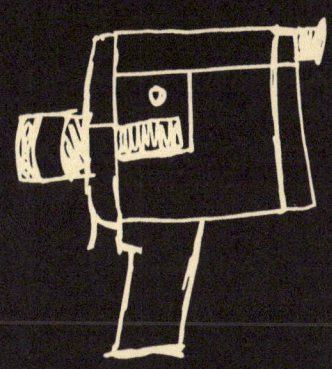

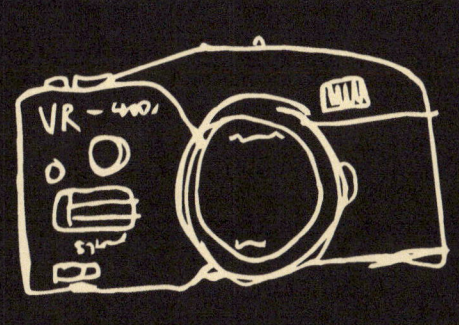

VR - 4400i

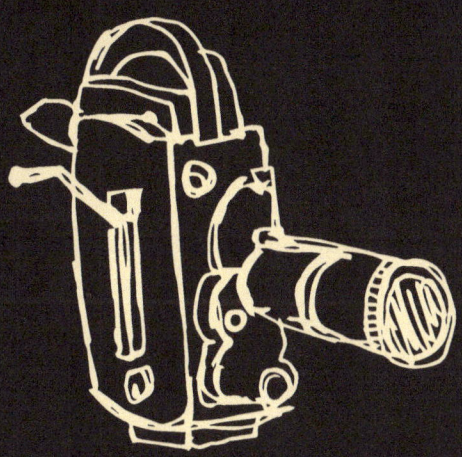

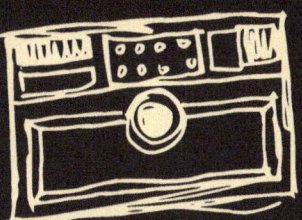

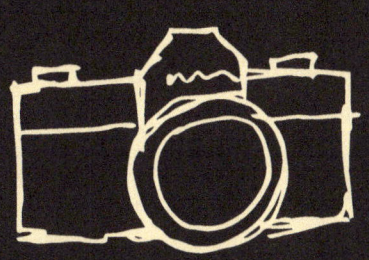

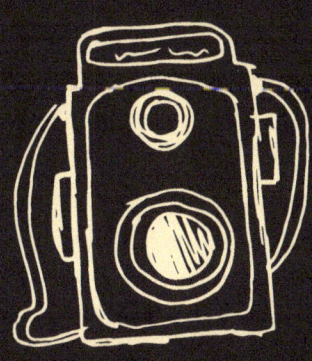

ARTISTS FEATURED

15_CHARLIE MIRADOR//UNTITLED (PHOTOGENIC)//MIXED MEDIA COLLAGE

Multidisciplinary artist working in painting, drawing, collage, and documentary photography. Based in San Francisco California.

16_FELIPE BELLOCQ//ALTIPLANO//8MM

Bachelor in Audiovisual Engineering with emphasis in image, also studied in Fine Arts University and the International Film School of Cuba. Together with Cine Casero Collective or freelance, I work on research and realization projects linked to the audiovisual archive. In shootings I have contributed so much with the camera and the light, as with the art and the scenography. For years I have participated as VJ with Mandinga Jazz band, but also in raves, performances, interventions, other shows and presentations. Along the way I have always been accompanied by my cameras and several rolls. In addition to, a passion for atmospheres and light. I enjoy experimenting with different emulsions and developing them manually. I appreciate the rhythm, I like the images and the movement.

18_AVANT KINEMA//FLOW STATE//SUPER 8MM

Scottish artists Sarahjane Swan & Roger Simian have collaborated since 2009 on a significant body of interdisciplinary works: analogue film, digital video, Indie songs, installation art, photography and experimental writing, most recently under the name Avant Kinema. The duo's experimental films - which often utilise long-expired filmstocks, which they process, handcraft and telecine at home–have screened around the World, from Europe and Scandinavia to Australia and both North and South America. Swan and Simian have created five full-scale installations and an Expanded Cinema Performance in the past eight years. They have received various arts grants and were awarded the Pauline Fay Lazarus Award for work based on human form in 2019, and were shortlisted for the Edinburgh International Film Festival's Short Film Challenge competition in 2016. Music by Swan and Simian has aired widely on BBC national radio and other stations, often as The Bird And The Monkey.

28_AZUCENA LOSANA//SELF (ALCHEMY)//RECIPE

Born and raised in Mexico City, 1977. I live and work in Buenos Aires, Argentina. My work is related to film making/developing, archive, film performace installations and video. I received the Third Prize of Arts and New Technologies from the Museum of Modern Art in Buenos Aires and Telefonica in 2009, the exchange scholarship of the University of Sao Paulo / UNA in 2015, and in 2016 a mention in the National Hall of Arts in Argentina. In 2017, I received the Creation Grant from the Nacional Arts Fund in Argentina and the grant for the Art Creators National System Program (SNCA) from the National Fund for Culture and the Arts (FONCA) in Mexico. My films have been screened at the Mar del Plata International Film Festival,

BAFICI, (S8) Mostra de Cinema Periferico, La Coruña, España, Kurzfilmtage in Oberhausen Germany, Los Angeles Filmforum's film series Ism, Ism, Ism: Experimental Cinema in Latin America, The Age d'Or Festival in Brussels, VIDEOEX in Zurich, Curta8 in Curitiba Brazil, PAF animation festival in Olomuc, Czech Republic, MEXPARIS MENTAL in France, the International Experimental Film Festival of Moscow MIEFF, the Week of the Experimental Film of La Plata - Argentina, UNCIPAR, among others.

32_BRITANY GUNDERSON//BACKGROUND MATERIAL//16MM

Britany Gunderson received a BFA in Film, Video, Animation, and New Genres at the University of Wisconsin-Milwaukee. Her practice is often interdisciplinary, creating film and video work that uses material forms such as hand-cut paper, textile fabrics, and celluloid. Exploring ideas of personal non-fiction, her work expands the idea of what a moving image can be. She has screened at venues internationally and received an Honorable Mention at the 2018 Milwaukee Underground Film Festival.

34_GABBY SUMNEY & HOGAN SEIDEL//SORROW SHARED//RECIPE

In the fall of 2018, Hogan Seidel and Gabby Sumney decided to tackle a yearly collaboration called Sorrow halved from the German idiom "Geteilte Freude ist doppelte Freude, geteilter Schmerz ist halber Schmerz." or "A sorrow shared, is a sorrow halved." The two queer artists took a shine to the idiom as they considered ways to subvert traditional notions of authorship and the experimental canon in their practice and their teaching. The "sorrow" of singular creative genius that is often hailed in the experimental world felt counter to the lessons they were bringing to their students and to their approach to making queer art.

Hogan & Gabby are both based in Boston, where they teach 16mm and experimental film. They both were interested in building pedagogical practices that incorporate collaborative modes of experimentation.

40_IGNACIO TAMARIT//THE CREATIVE USE OF TAPES//RECIPE

Ignacio Tamarit (1991, Buenos Aires, Argentina) is a filmmaker, teacher and archivist who received his diploma in film preservation and audiovisual restoration from the Universidad de Buenos Aires (UBA) in 2019. He studied at the Centro de Investigación Cinematográfica and at the Facultad de Filosofía y Letras, Universidad de Buenos Aires. He has given film workshops at Big Sur Galería de Arte Contemporáneo, C3 Centro Cultural de la Ciencia, L'Etna (France), Les Météorites (France) and Lumiton Museo del Cine Usina Audiovisual, where he also works as an archivist and curator. His films have been exhibited at Museo de Arte Contemporáneo de Mar del Plata (Argentina), Centro Cultural San Martin (Argentina), Palais de Glace (Argentina) Onion City Film Festival (USA), LaborBerlin (Germany), L'Etna (France), Unza Lab (Italy), Slamdance Film Festival (USA), Festival Internacional de Cine de Mar del Plata (Argentina) BAFICI (Argentina) Edinburgh International Film Festival (Escocia), (S8) Mostra de Cinema Periférico (España), Exis Experimental Film And Video Festival (Corea), Festival Internacional de Cine Lima Independiente (Perú), Antimatter Media Art (Canadá), Curta 8 (Brazil), Los Angeles Film Forum (USA), Österreichisches Filmmuseum (Austria), L' ge d'Or (Bélgium), Linoleum Festival of Contemporary Animation and Media Art (Ukraine) among others.

44_IVAN SALOMÃO E NAYANA FERREIRA//O AMOR É UMA ATO REVOLUCIONÁRIO//SUPER 8MM

Flight instructor as profession and analog filmmaker as passion. Super8 was the way to know analog film and the lab is the place where the magic comes from!

46_KEVIN FERMINI//VIOLA VS. THE VAMPIRE KING//SUPER 8MM

Director, DP and editor in Atlanta.

52_LAUREN HENSCHEL LAUREN HENSCHEL//INFUSION NO. 1//16MM

Lauren Henschel (b.1992) is a visual artist working primarily in hand-processed 16mm film, installation and performance. Her work interrogates questions around guilt, illness, disability, shame and mortality and seeks to defy or alter an audience's expectations and experience of what art can reveal about the experience of inhabiting a body. Born and raised in Miami, Florida, Lauren is currently based in Durham, N.C. Her work has been displayed at numerous venues, including Carnegie Hall and the Miami Art Museum. She holds a B.A. in Visual Media Studies from Duke University. This spring, she received an MFA in Experimental and Documentary Arts from Duke University.

56_NOLAN BARRY//UNTITLED (CAR AND ROAD)//35MM

Nolan Barry is an experimental filmmaker and artist whose work is based around ideas of perception, looking to light as a vessel for understanding reality. Nolan lives in Chicago, Illinois and is currently studying at the School of the Art Institute of Chicago. Nolan's works on 16mm aim to capture light in a way that is true to the phenomenon of reflection. His work utilizes the unique opportunity to harness and distort light provided by the physicality of film. Living in a digitized and internet-based society, Nolan turns to film as a medium to capture, archive, and replicate the light of a specific moment in time and space.

58_PABLO MARTINEZ-ZARATE//COCHINEAL IN ANALOG FILM PHOTOGRAPHY//RECIPE

Pablo Martinez-Zarate is a media artist and researcher that works in the intersection of film, interactive narrative and photography. He is in charge of the dark room at Universidad Iberoamericana in Mexico City, where he leads the Iberoamerican Documentary Lab and the Master in Film. He uses analog processes in many works, and responding to his interest in narrative innovation, he builds bridges between analog media, radical aesthetics and immersive narratives (such as super 8 based VR). His films have received awards internationally and he has held solo shows in some of the main museums in Mexico City, as well as important independent spaces. Pablo is considered to be one of the pioneers in webdocumentary in Mexico and has been guest lecturer and speaker in places such as EICTV San Antonio de los Baños in Cuba, Emerson College Boston, University of Southern Califonia L.A., Zurich University of the Arts, among others.

62_ROBERT C. BANKS//35MM STILLS

Robert Banks is an experimental filmmaker, freelance cinematographer, and teacher of filmmaking and photography. One of Bank's best-known works is the 1992 short film *X: The Baby Cinema*, which chronicles the commercial appropriation and transformation of Malcolm X into a commodity-image. His 1995 documentary film, *You Can't Get a Piece of Mind*, explores the world of Cleveland musician and Vietnam War veteran Dan "Supie T" Theman. Banks' films have been screened at the Sundance Film Festival, SXSW Film-Music Festival, Film Festival Rotterdam, the New York Underground Film Festival, Chicago Underground Film Festival, the Ann Arbor Film Festival, and the Cleveland International Festival Festival. He is recipient of numerous awards, including Filmmaker of the Year at the Midwest Filmmakers Conference in 2001 and featured filmmaker for the BBC British Short Film Festival (2000). Banks currently teaches at New Bridge Center for Art and Technology, films corporate training videos, and works on all aspects of cinematography for filmmaker-colleagues and clients throughout the country. Some of his films include MPG: Motion Picture Genocide, My First Drug, The Idiot Box, Jaded, Outlet, Embryonic, Goldfish and Sunflowers, AWOL, Autopilot, and Faith in Chaos, all of which are shot and edited on 16/35 mm film. Banks attended the Cleveland School of the Arts, the Cleveland Institute of Art, the Ohio School of Broadcasting, and Cleveland State University. He also served one term overseas in the U.S. Air Force. He taught film and photography at Cuyahoga Community College, the Cleveland Institute of Art, and Cleveland State University.

64_MATT SOAR//THE LOST LEADERS PROJECT//ESSAY

Matt Soar is a Montreal-based intermedia artist and filmmaker. His work is often to be found at the intersection of residual and emergent media forms and practices. *Lost Leaders* is an archival, interpretive exploration of the histories and aesthetics of US/Canadian film leader standards since 1930. Outcomes since 2011 include: photomontage, stained glass, interactive films and installations, handpainted, handwritten, and handwoven films, stopmotion animation, and, microvideography. Soar's films have screened at ATA/Other Cinema, Montreal Underground Film Festival, Orphan Film Symposium, Rencontre internationales du documentaire de Montréal, VISONS Montreal, and the Engauge Experimental Film Festival.

68_RACHEL GUARDIOLA//INTO THE ZONE (ANTHOLOGY OF ACCOUNTS FINDINGS)//16MM

Rachel Guardiola is an interdisciplinary artist and naturalist with a studio practice that focuses on analog and digital lens based technology. Her work explores the human relationship to wilderness through the construction of other earths, mythologies inspired by periods of solitary navigation through extreme landscapes. She utilizes photography, film, video, sound, alternative processes, performance, and installation to reimagine topographies free of human presence. Science fiction and the fantastic are utilized as a mode to discuss environmental realities. The works playfully teeter between fact and fiction to become environments of the uncanny.

72_ROBYN EHRLICH//SNAPSHOTS//16MM

Robyn Ehrlich is a film and video artist from Eagan, Minnesota, and a recent graduate from the Department of Film, Video, Animation, and New Genres at the University of Wisconsin - Milwaukee. In her work, she maintains a focus on themes such as feminism, the female experience, and body positivity.

74_RITA HARPER//ARTIST PROFILE//35MM

Rita Harper is a documentary photographer/photojournalist from Atlanta, Georgia. She first became interested in imagery at a young age where her quiet nature allowed her to be more observant to the world around her. With no formal art education, she began to take to the streets of Atlanta and discover a style of her own. She quickly realized the affinity she had for capturing black life and Atlanta culture simultaneously. Film photography became a quick obsession as it fit the raw unfiltered aesthetic of her work.

Her hometown Atlanta had become the New Hollywood of the South and people from other cities were migrating for new opportunity. While this was amazing and progressive, the aboriginals to the city and original culture were not being captured respectfully. It is her goal to show the beauty of the everyday person, and that you don't have to be a celebrity to have value. Rita hopes to show the diversity and cover the subcultures of black life. She also loves to capture up close and intimate portraits that capture raw emotion and feeling.

84_ROGER HORN//SCENES FROM A TRANSIENT HOME//SUPER 8MM

Roger Horn is an unconventional filmmaker and post-doctoral research associate at Freie Universität Berlin in the Visual & Media Anthropology MA program. His PhD in Social Anthropology, "Memories, material culture, and methodology: Employing multiple filmic formats, forms, and informal archives in anthropological research among Zimbabwean migrant women" included several accompanying films which have screened widely at festival such as the 65th International Short Film Festival Oberhausen, 2020 Clermont-Ferrand International Short Film Festival, and the 21st & 22nd Ji.hlava International Documentary Film Festivals.

88_SARAH SEENÉ//LUMEN//SUPER 8MM

Sarah Seené is a photographer and filmmaker who works with analog media (35mm, 120mm, Polaroid, Super8). Bringing together mainly portraits, her images focus on faces, bodies and the human being. The photographic material offered by the film has allowed her to develop a singular poetry, a dream that animates each of her series. Her work is inspired by the concept of resilience and the capacity to be reborn from ashes.

92_GUILLAUME VALLÉE//GRAND-MAMAN PIANO//SUPER 8MM

Experimental filmmaker, video artist and independant curator, Guillaume Vallée graduated from Concordia University with a Major in Film Animation and MFA in Studio Arts, Film Production. He's interested in alternative forms of moving images in analogue forms as a way of considering the direct interaction between different mediums. His work is an exploration of materiality within the creative process. In attempts of creating a more complex relationship with his subject matter, Vallée makes use of cross-medium forms that range from camera-less techniques to optical effects, glitch, video feedback, resulting in expended & hybrid pieces. He works mainly on Super8, 16mm and VHS.

Vallée is questioning the notions of recycling & reappropriation, treating all material as found footage within a collaborative practice, in film, video & performance. His audiovisual performances have been shown in various festivals in Canada, USA, France, Italy and Japan and his experimental films and videos, distributed by Vidéographe and Winnipeg Film Group, have been screened internationaly.

His work has been awarded in 2013, for The Yellow Ghost (Grand Prix Dérapage), in 2016 at the WNDX festival (Festival of Moving Image) for his short film, Le bulbe tragique ('' Best Canadian Work '') and il fait gris dans ta tête, tout à coup, a videopoem codirected with Sarah Seené, as part of Festival de Poésie de Montréal (Grand Prix Video-Poésie 2018).

Guillaume Vallée has been an artist-in-residence at La Bande Vidéo (Quebec, Canada) in 2017 and at Le Fresnoy - studio national des arts contemporains (Tourcoing, FR) & Signal Culture (Owego, USA) in 2018. He's currently an artist-in-residence at Main Film, part of the Film Factory program (2019-2020).

94_SCOTT LAZER//COMMUTE//16MM

Scott Lazer is a filmmaker and creative director whose repertoire transcends genres, formats, and media. He has directed original programming for HBO, Spotify, and Tidal, amongst others. His work has been nominated for MTV Video Music Awards and screened at film festivals around the world. His collaborations with artists such as J. Cole, Daniel Caesar, Tierra Whack, BJ The Chicago Kid, Ari Lennox, J.I.D, Thundercat, and Bas have given him the opportunity to work with talent such as Kevin Hart and Ansel Elgort while telling stories through a unique cultural lens that depicts a style that is all his own.

98_TOM SCHULTE//BETWEEN TWO WORLDS: A GUIDE ON MULTI-EXPOSING SUPER 8MM FILM//RECIPE

Tom Schulte is an Australian creative, self taught in photography, film-making, and writing. 'DIY' is one of the main motives when working with film, and whilst he enjoys shooting and hand-developing 35mm, 16mm, and Super 8mm in alternative processing, Tom also experiments with various projection methods and carries out basic repairs/maintenance on cameras, lenses, projectors, and editors. Tom regularly writes poems, and occasionally combines both spoken words and film to create a singular piece of work or performance.

102_ZOE GRACE MARQUEDANT//STUDYING DEGRADATION IN DISASTER//ESSAY

Zoe Grace Marquedant is a writer and journalist from Rockville, Maryland. She received her B.A. in Creative Writing from Sarah Lawrence College and her M.F.A. in Nonfiction from Columbia University. Her work primarily focuses on questions of time, art, conservation, and responsibility. She has been published by SLCSpeaks, the Columbia Journal online, Untitled Magazine, Distanzin, Fathom Press, and others. She also has essays forthcoming in Manque and The School of Commons. She is currently one of the 2020 artists in residence at the Dogo Residenz für Neue Kunst in Lichtensteig, Switzerland. She otherwise works as a freelance creator and editor.

106_ROXY BEAT//ARTIST PROFILE//35MM AND 120MM

Rossana Battisti (born 1978, Terni, Italy) is a visual artist working primarily with analogue cameras.
She defines her photograph an emotional photograph and her works have a strong evocative power.
Rossana photographs the dream, the invisible and the unconscious. Her photographic experiments are intimate and conceptual, the self-portraits decline her to the third person and the journey is for her a reflection on life. Her works are mostly autobiographical, symbolic and twilight poetry and nature are some of the elements that make up his works.
In the world of photography is Roxy Beat.

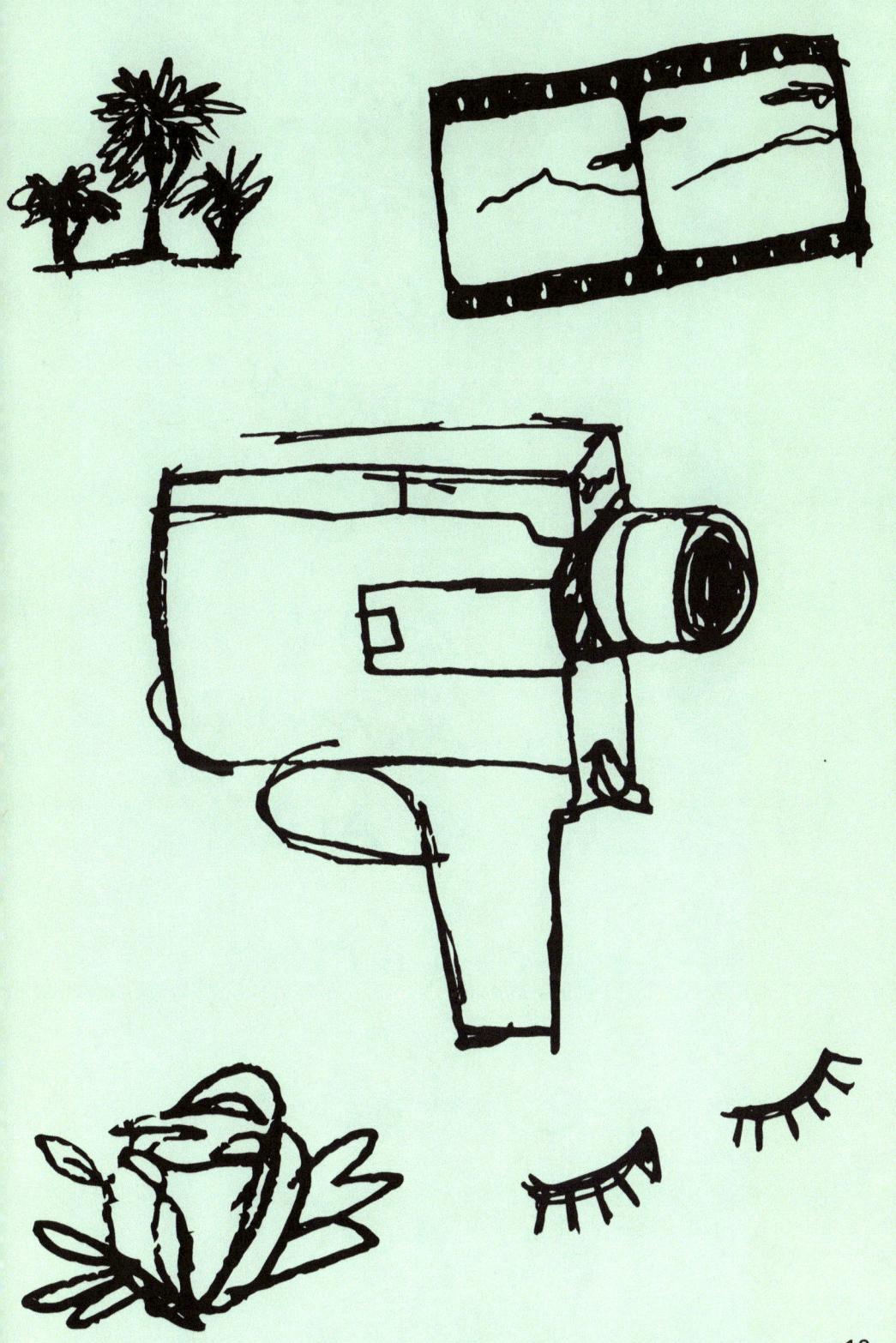

TRY AGAIN

TRY AGAIN

TRY AGAIN

TRY AGAIN

TRY AGAIN

TRY AGAIN

TRY AGAIN

TRY AGAIN

TRY AGAIN

TRY AGAIN

TRY AGAIN

Charlie Mirador

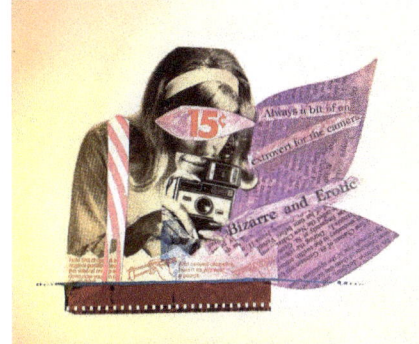 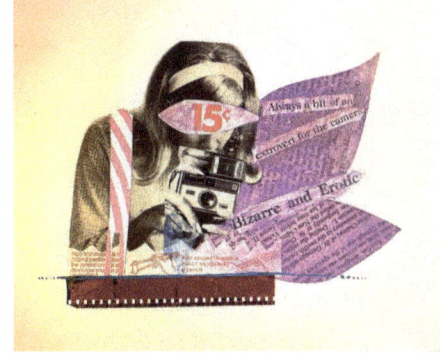

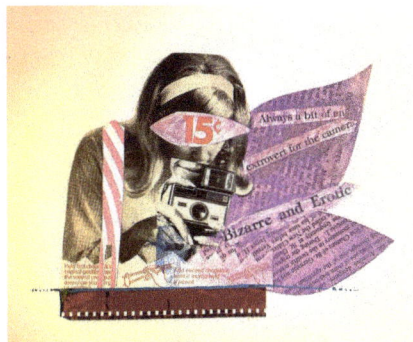 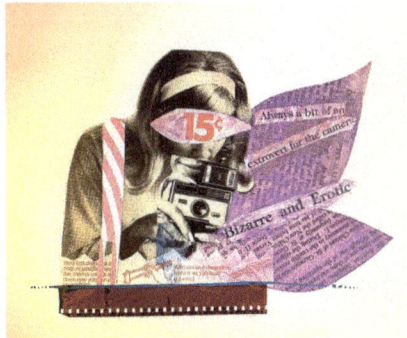

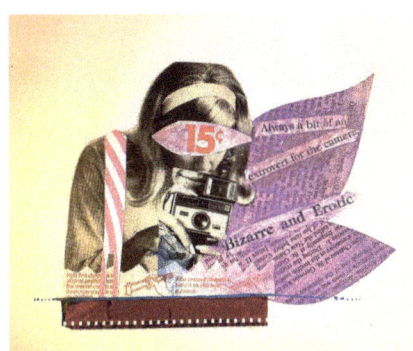 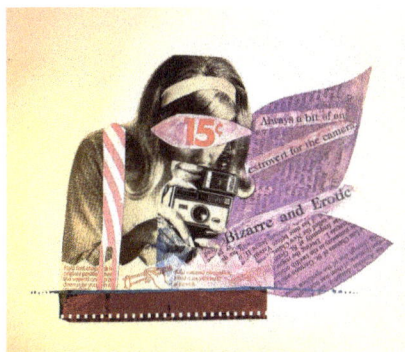

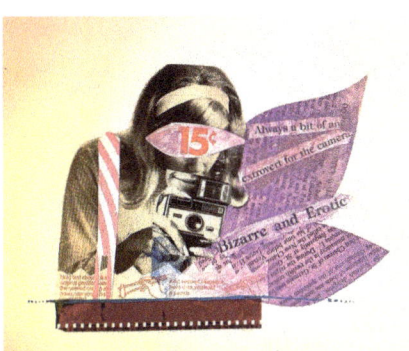 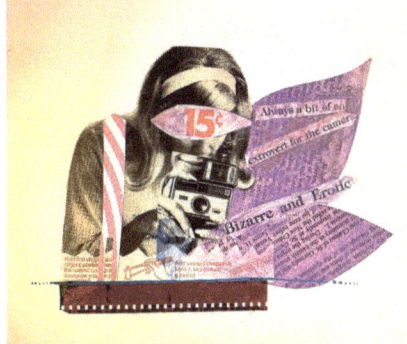

FELIPE   BELLOCQ

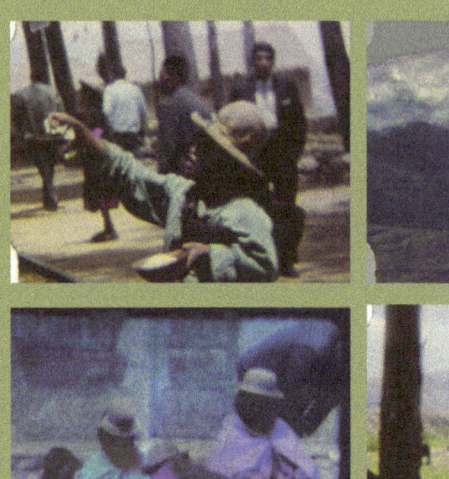
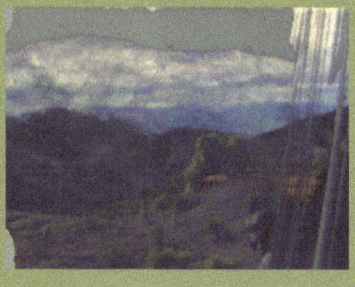
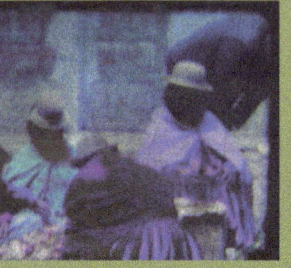
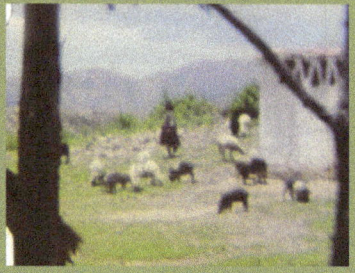

TELL US A BIT ABOUT YOUR BACKGROUND IN AUDIOVISUAL ENGINEERING.

Audiovisual Engineering is a really diverse career, so i think everyone gives it his own focus. In my case I started to shoot film photography while I was studying and also working at the University Film Archive. At the same time I started some VJing projects in collaboration with DJs and jazz bands. After that I started to shoot on film and develop myself. Audiovisual engineering gave me some interesting ways to approach some workflows, methods and knowledge. I was able to shoot, develop, digitalize, edit and project my short films.

What inspired you to create Altiplano?

Altiplano was conceived really fermentally, during my work as audiovisual archive researcher and producer for the documentary movie *Fattoruso*. Directed by Santiago Bednarik, this biopic portrays Hugo Fattoruso's life and music career. At that time I had privileged access to his incredible personal archive materials. I was easily attracted by the 8mm film collection that is really diverse and shows his years with the band "Los Shakers". All those images made me travel through time and space to the 60's in Bolivia and Peru, and reminded me of some backpacker trips I had made some years ago in those landscapes. Also being in contact with Hugo was really inspiring, appreciating his wisdom, energy and music. All these backgrounds were perfect for the psychedelic style of the film too.

In some ways this is a film about Los Shakers on tour, but you choose not to focus on the band members. What informed this decision?
I felt really connected and attracted by the images had chosen, almost instantaneously. Also I wanted to focus on their alternative eye, I mean there are a lot of typically rock band images, like they doing things for the camera or just playing. However I also recognized that there were some rolls that show a really different point of view, with attention on other things like the people, society and culture of those places. I feel that it is actually interesting to imagine young kids that, thanks to their success and fame, were able to travel through Latin America discovering new realities, playing and shooting film.

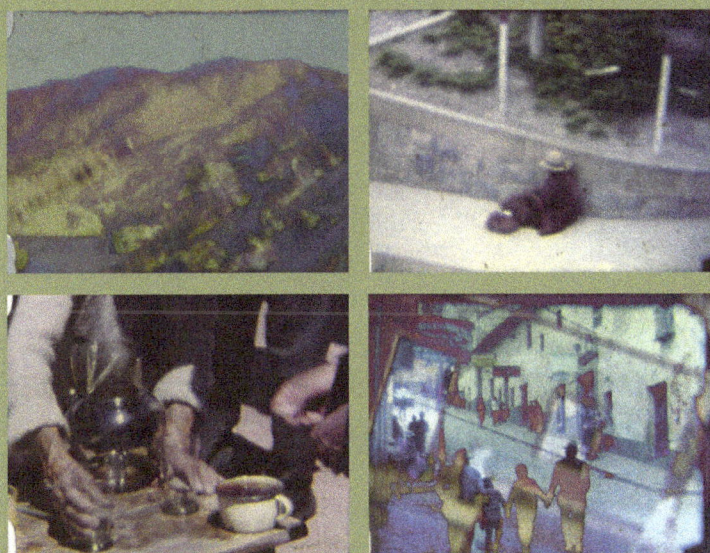

How much footage were you working with?

The total number of 8mm original film rolls is 33 rolls, almost all are 50ft length. All of them are in really great condition, so we were able to project and film them with a digital camera to make a telecine digital file. Then I made a selection and digitalized frame-by-frame hi-res 4 of them to edit *Altiplano*.

Why was it important to work with an archive of 8mm film?

I think that the importance of archives in general lies mostly on its access and diffusion. In that way, doing kind of found-footage project is a manner of bringing back to life at least for a while to some of these materials. Sometimes I think about how many incredible images are stored in archives or collections without seeing the light for decades. Working with old materials is also important for their preservation and because it keeps the technology and wisdom alive.

Personally I love the 8mm format, its tininess and how powerful it is besides it. I think it is the format that at that time allowed lots of people who couldn't shoot on 16mm for different reasons but they could do it on 8mm and give us incredible images of their trips and adventures as it is much more portable.

Have any other film projects on the horizon?

I'm starting the pre-production of a 16mm portrait of my 94 years old grandmother and her house. I'm also planning to finish the trilogy in collaboration with Jorge Gamarra, with whom I have already made part one *Estuario* and two *Confluencia* both in Super 8mm.

For the next months I have both 16mm and Super8mm Workshops scheduled for the University and as freelance in collaboration with Silvana Camors and Anton Terni.

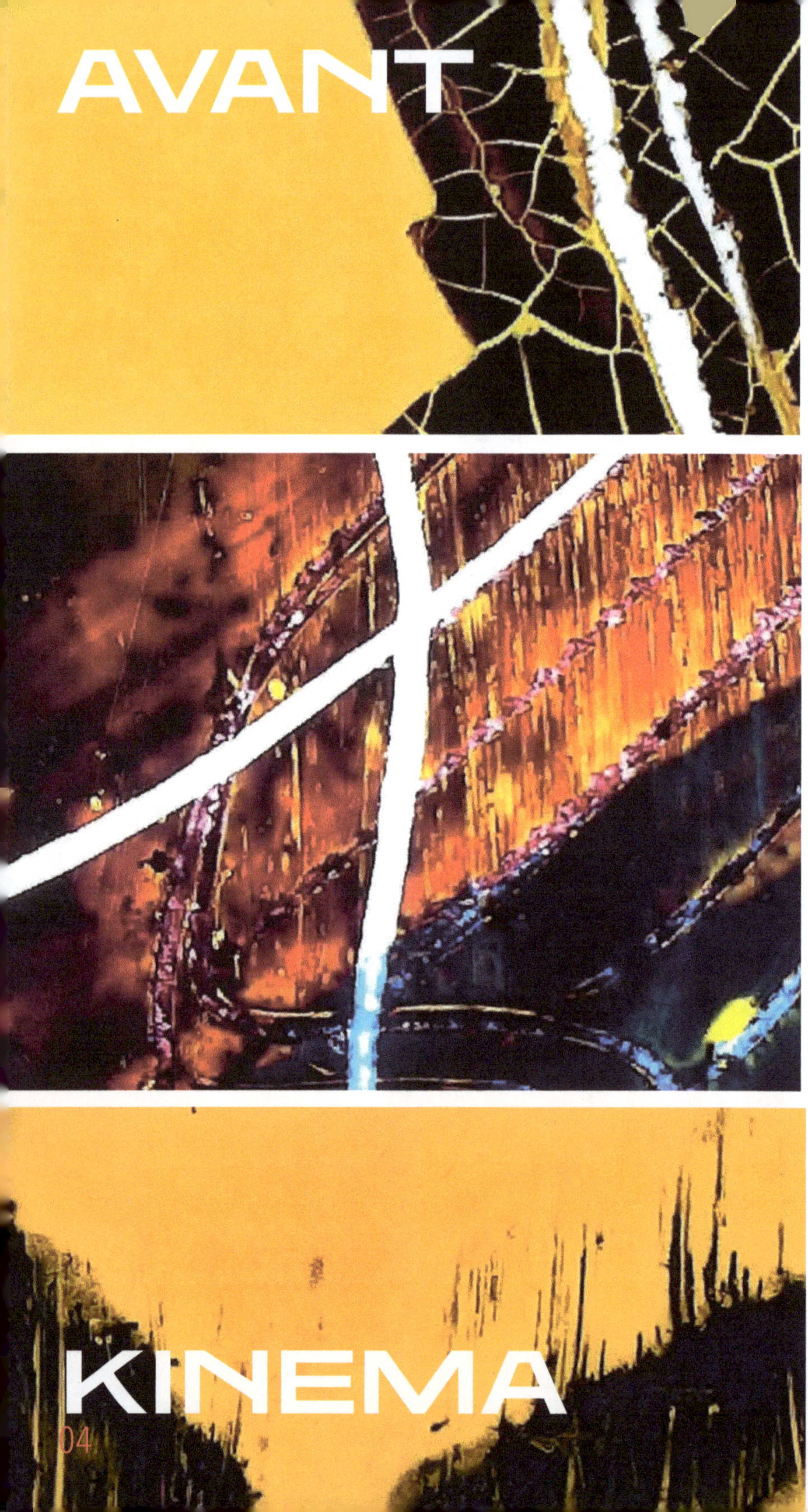

AVANT

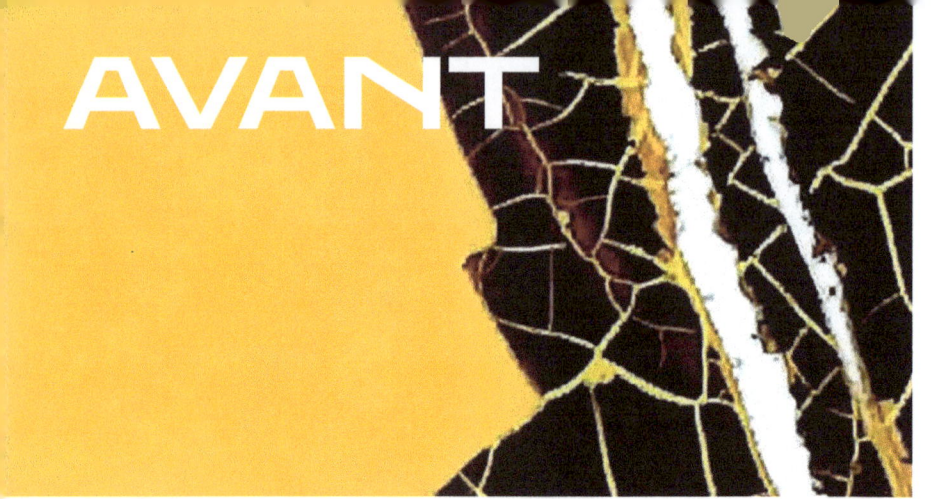

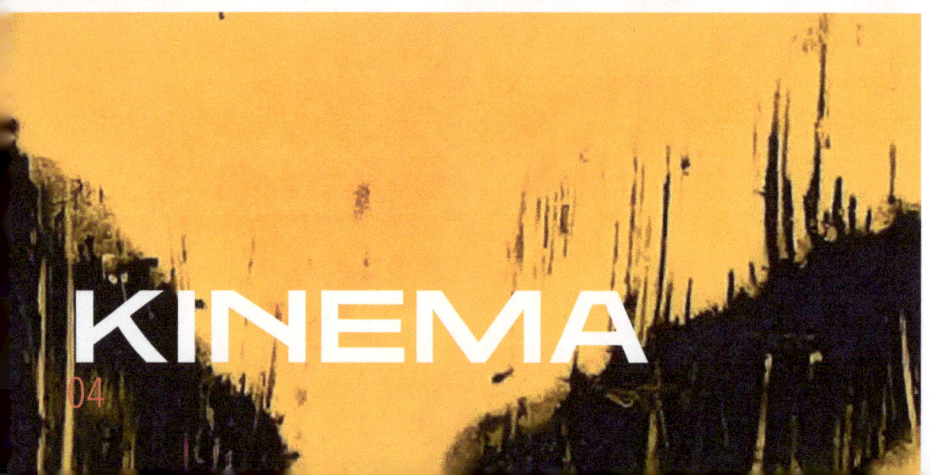

KINEMA

04

TELL US ABOUT AVANT KINEMA...

FLOW STATE (Handcrafted Series no. 1) is an experimental handcrafted Super 8 film. The film features one cartridge of vintage Super 8 film-stock, with each frame scratched and painstakingly colored by hand.

Sarahjane Swan & Roger Simian: Thank you for inviting us into the Analog Cookbook fold. Because we're Scottish we spell everything with a quirky European twist: Programme, Colour, Neighbourhood, Analogue.

Sarahjane: Avant Kinema is the name Roger and I now use for all the different strands of collaborative work we make together: experimental film, music, art, installation work, expanded cinema performances, photography and writing. We love the mix of "avant", which always seems to point to the future, alongside "kinema", which is a very old-fashioned term and spelling of the word.

Roger: Having those two words crushed up together seems to hint that we're drawing from the past at the same time as looking forwards into the unknown. We always like to approach things from many angles at once. We wrote an Artist Manifesto a few years ago which states that "as creators we're mostly interested in the polymathic, the multi-dimensional. Through our collaboration we're striving towards artworks made up of multiple forms: the cinematic, the musical, the sculptural, the literary, the photographic and the immersive. We are one woman and one man, existing in time and place, our sensors set to record. We want to record this world from every angle, but a world can never be known objectively. It can only be remembered, dreamed, imagined, fantasized, glimpsed in the shadows, reflected and distorted in the swirl and tug of an ocean... We want a Total Art through which we can piece together all those gathered fragments and parts into meaningful representations of the World as seen in the splinters and shards of a smashed mirror".

Sarahjane: This mixing together of different art forms is most obvious in our installations, which usually involve multiple projections, music, sculptural works and written elements all working together to tell a story. But even in a film such as "Flow State" the music will often have as important a role to play as the images do.

How did both of you first get into working tactilly with celluloid?

Roger: We've always loved the analogue look and, because our digital filmmaking and music videos often tended to have a very experimental, DIY, Lo-Fi edge - messing around with colour and superimposed elements - I guess we were always striving for an aesthetic with a similar atmosphere and texture to the analogue work we've always loved. We weren't consciously trying to fake it with faux light-leaks or grain or superimposed scratches, or anything like that. We only did that once, with a one minute film, "Somnambulance", which screened across the Toronto Subway Network as part of the T.U.F.F. festival, and that was really just a one-off: a stepping stone towards us trying it out for real. We finally took the plunge in 2016 after watching the Super 8 feature, "Silver", by the Canadian filmmaker, Allan Brown, at the Alchemy Film and Moving Image Festival, which we thought was great. We did all the online research we could, bought a Canon 514XL for £27 and an AGFA Family camera and projector for £53, both from eBay, and ordered a cartridge each of TRI-X black and white and Vision3 colour film, shot them and sent them off to a professional lab (Gauge Film) for processing and HD digital scans. The Vision3 ended up a bit too overexposed and washed out but we were blown away by the stark, high contrast look of the TRI-X

analogue to us is like a whole organic tactile sensory wonderland

and we edited our footage into a short film inspired the the late '70s New York No Wave cinema, which we called "Superfly Super 8 circa Nineteen Seventy-Seven". That was our first ever Super 8 film and it opened doors for us, so we definitely had the bug then. We realized though that to buy a cartridge of modern S8 film-stock and get it professionally processed and scanned costs over a hundred pounds a go. We just couldn't afford to keep forking out that much money for 3 minutes 20 seconds of footage. So we found out all about buying up cheap long-expired vintage Kodachrome 40 cartridges in bulk and processing these at home using household ingredients.

If you search Youtube for "avant kinema hand-processing caffenol" you should find the step-by-step guide we made for processing Super 8 film using the Caffenol recipe: coffee, washing soda and vitamin c.

Sarahjane: I think film became a very tangible thing to us once we started exploring using different cameras and stock, then learning to process the film ourselves. After feeling through the whole process - shoot / process / project - we just fell in love with the results. Actually holding film, watching frames appear before your eyes as the chemicals do their trick. It was like an Alchemical Magic and now we just can't look back.

Processing film can be very powerful. A bit nerve-racking when you first start. You have an expired cartridge and need to work out how to pull 50ft of film out of it in the dark without it snapping or getting scratched. Then you're needing to accurately measure out all the ingredients and mix them up with the correct timings and temperatures. And there's always the worry about whether you'll even see any images at the end of it all. Will your projector chew up and spit out the film? We've had that happen! But when it works out well it's a major rush. This is what experimentation is all about: putting yourself out there to possibly fail. Learning that even your failures can be reworked into successes. The glory and excitement and often unpredictable beauty that can come from working directly with actual celluloid is unbeatable. From a film that was a ghost - it had almost no purpose, sitting expired, unwanted and undeveloped - now transformed into a tangible piece of art!

Digital has all its good points too, but analogue to us is like a whole organic tactile sensory wonderland! Digital can sometimes feel a bit stuffy, pre-meditated and conventional. What you get is what you shoot only. Often the magic is done in post-production. With analogue the magic happens in the camera, on the film and in the processing or handcrafting. So you can't help getting hands-on tactile and involved when dealing with actual film. I trained as a Fine Art Sculptor so this way of working seems very familiar to me. To work directly with film - to feel it running through your fingers - seems a very natural and creative way of producing work.

We're not purists. We will mix both analogue and digital together, as that is experimenting to us. All formats and ideas and tools are for creating but they do all have very different looks and experiences

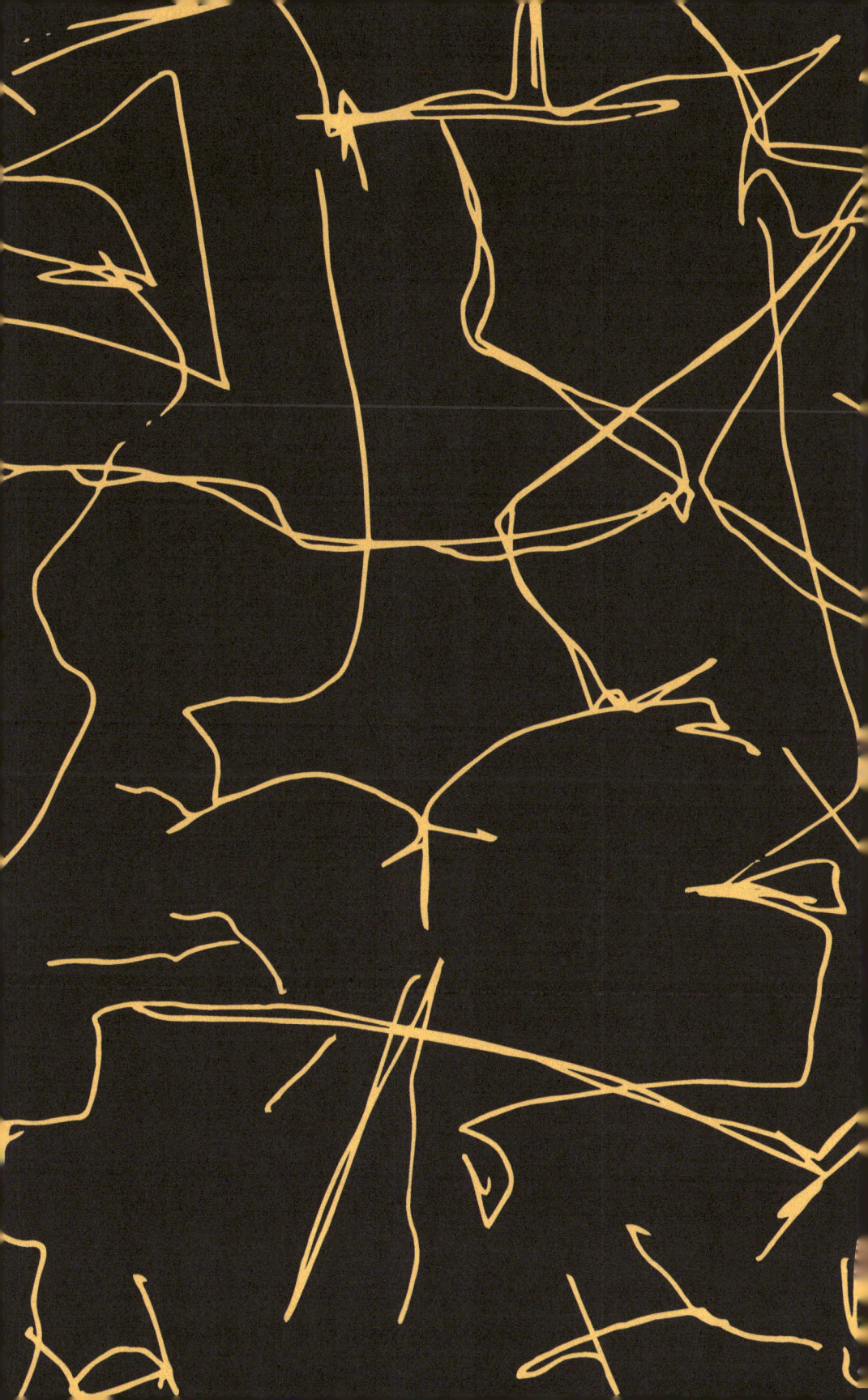

attached to them. Working with analogue film - especially the process of handcrafting, colouring and scratching or manipulating the film in other ways - adds that whole tactile, sensory, sculptural element, which just enriches the whole experience.

Roger: We were also very aware that people were handcrafting film in different ways and coming up with lots of interesting camera-less techniques. Directly painting and scratching and adding other adornments. Or burying the film amongst rotten fruit and vegetables to see how the chemical changes affect the images. Or distressing it with bleach and other abrasive substances. I downloaded and started reading through Helen Hill's excellent 'zine - "Recipes For Disaster: a Handcrafted Film Cookbooklet" - about all the different creative and experimental ways we can work directly with film. Coming from a DIY / fanziney background I thought it was great that the contributions from all the various filmmakers were so personal and individualized: some typed up, some handwritten or drawn in underground comic styles. Having got to know Helen Hill virtually, through her contributions to that booklet and some of her own film work, which I tracked down online, it was very sad to later read how she had passed away. I'm sure she would be making great work still today. We both love the way that Analog Cookbook helps keep the spirit of her booklet alive.

So, meanwhile - as I was engrossed in reading up on camera-less filmmaking techniques - Sarahjane was busy just getting on with it. She got hold of a light box and a jeweller's eye so that she could closely study each individual tiny Super 8 image while she was working on it. She also put together a fun box full of sharpie pens, scissors and scrapers, glittery nail-varnish, tiny stickers and other assorted products and items that she still uses for her handcrafting experiments. I'm planning to also try out some camera-less / handcrafting techniques myself for one of our future projects.

Tell us a bit about how the concept of a flow state influenced this film

Roger: Sarahjane had actually already crafted the cartridge of Super 8 and we were watching it back.

It still had no sound. We were trying to decide what exactly we were looking at.

Sarahjane: It looked like thousands of abstract painting canvases which had somehow sparked into movement. From my original experience of working on each individual 8mm frame this thing had become wildly animated and taken on a whole life of its own. I found my eyes playing tricks on me. There were unexpected changes in direction, where a shape or object which should be going downwards or to the right now seemed to move upwards or to the left.

Roger: While we were watching we were excited by what we were seeing and we started throwing ideas around for a possible title and a theme. Sarahjane felt strongly that any title should include the word "flow", because of the ways the images moved. We did a search around that word and found our way to Mihály Csíkszentmihályi's 1970s theories on the Flow State.

Sarahjane: I couldn't believe how apt this was. His theories seemed to totally capture that same frame of mind I'm in whenever I'm crafting film. I'm sure that any of your readers who have tried out handcrafting film for themselves will have experienced the Flow State.

Roger: Watching the film back again, with that concept strongly in mind, it really felt to both of us that viewers might also enter a Flow State while they were taking in and trying to process or make sense of these fairly abstract moving images.

There's such a strong connection between music and the visuals here. Which came first? What does that process look like?

Roger: All of these ideas and feelings relating to the concept of the Flow State were flowing through us when we got into composing the soundtrack. As we mentioned earlier, the images were created first when Sarahjane handcrafted the film. Having used our Winait telecine machine to made a digital copy, we then experimented with playing this back at different speeds until we found the pace that seemed to flow the best. We wanted it to be fast moving but for the brain to still be able to take

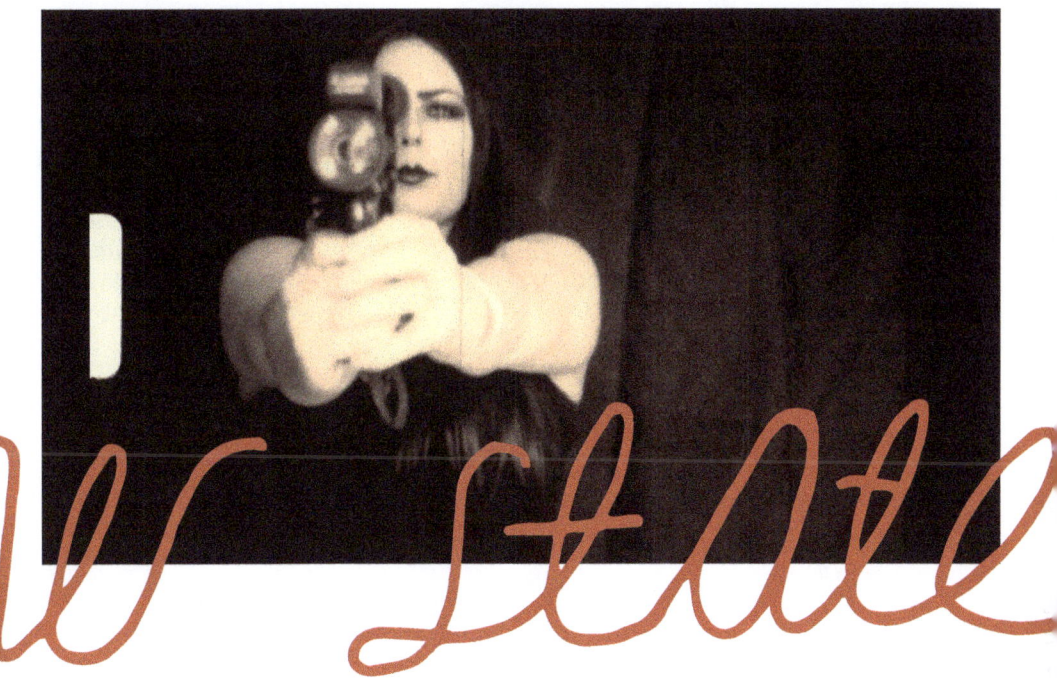

in each individual image rather than just being confronted with a dizzying blur.

Then, once we had the concept of the Flow State in mind, we decided to create a soundtrack which seemed full of sparks and energy, like the embodiment of an electrical flow. This process mostly involved us both improvising to a pre-recorded rhythm track with heavily detuned guitars. We were going for that balance between melody and discordance that you hear in a lot of Sonic Youth's music. We are both big fans of the albums "Daydream Nation" and "Sister" and felt that something in that vein, but with our own personality stamped on it, would work with that imagery. Creating those droney, hypnotic, wild and free-flowing sounds certainly made us both feel we had entered the Flow State. We were so lost in creating the music that time and place and anything else outside of that moment seemed to slip away. I'm sure that the more freeform jazz musicians - from Miles Davis and John Coltraine to Albert Ayler and Sun Ra - must have regularly entered this same altered state of mind, and not just because of whichever illicit subsctances they had consumed either. No, the Flow State streams directly from creative practice.

What materials did you use to scratch and paint the film?

Sarahjane: The scratches are made up with a small pair of cuticle scissors which have a small curve at the ends. This allows straight and curved lines and I can use the actual point or the side curve to make different marks. I use a jeweller's eyepiece so I can see as much detail as possible. I use a light box to illuminate the film so I can get a clear view of the film. All these tools help me to have a better idea of what I'm looking at and what I'm creating. Sometimes I really want to create a definite mark and repeat marks too and sometimes I want to just impulsively score and scratch with abandon to feel an energy flowing through the movement. Some movements and marks speak to me, so and I feel a definite connection has been made, so I can confidently make the next marks almost in connection to each other. Some marks are made passionately with one long score or extended movement. I might leave them as they are or I may go back to the long scratch and add to it with detail of more movement. A kind of layering effect and some scratches are just that: an impulsive movement, a kind of knowing, always moving and flowing forwards, and back like a tide or a wave.

I will always try out new materials to experiment with but the ones I've used so far include: Sharpie pens, ink, paint, nail varnish, varnish, eye-liner pens, nail varnish with glitter in it, glue with plastic in it and acetate pens.

I'm starting to experiment with nail varnish remover and a kind of smudging effect using a cotton bud. I can layer colours and then remove parts to create different effects and visuals. I have also started working with some found footage for the first time. In the past I've always worked with more or less blank film, where I'm creating with a blank canvas, but the found footage has a whole different feel to it.. I'm looking at images and a narrative already in place and it is very interesting to process all of these elements together. Different questions are being asked of myself as I want to explore the images and maybe alter some to almost create a new story or narrative. It is very exciting.

What film stock did you use?

Roger: For this first film in our series of 100% Handcrafted films we picked a cartridge of Kodachrome 40. We had already shot footage on this and processed it ourselves using the Caffenol recipe (coffee, washing soda, vitamin c) but it was one of those experiments which hadn't worked out at all well. All we could see were scratches and blotches and vague forms without any distinctive features. That's always disheartening but the beauty of experimenting with Super 8 is that any home-processing failures can be added to the "Film-stock for Scratching Up" pile.

Whenever we can afford to we like to buy up batches of long-expired Kodachrome 40 on eBay. They're relatively inexpensive and, because K40 can no longer be processed as colour film, there are thousands of them just sitting there languishing in dust in people's attics or under beds without purpose. We keep a batch of these stocked up in the bottom of our fridge because they are ideal for messing around with. One of our most successful films, "Boy And The Sea" - which screened at the Royal Scottish Academy and won the Pauline Fay Lazarus Prize for Work Using the Human Form - captures our son, Nico, who has autism, playing in the sea. This was shot on Ayr beachfront on a couple of cartridges of Kodachrome 40 which had passed their use-by dates in the mid-1980s. If a film like "Boy And The Sea" had been shot and processed at the time it would have had the beauty of all that rich Kodachrome colour, which is really what we're recognizing when we think of 20th Century analogue cinema. The way it exists now, however, has a different kind of beauty: a much more melancholy monochrome ghostly fragility which perfectly matches the theme of our film which is all about memory, and being alive, and Nico's sensory experience of the Sea.

We also have a few long-expired Ektachrome cartridges and an E6 chemistry kit. We've bought a Sous Vide precision cooker especially so that we can regulate the temperatures as it's supposed to be a very tricky process. We've spent so long processing in monochrome with Caffenol that we're excited to try out some colour processing.

Then for other films - when we've wanted a crisper, richer look made up of higher contrasts - we've used modern Super 8 film-stocks, such as Kodak TRI-X B&W Reversal Film and we've paid a professional lab (Gauge Film) to do the processing and make up an HD digital scan.

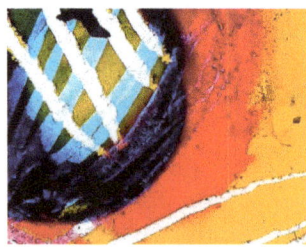
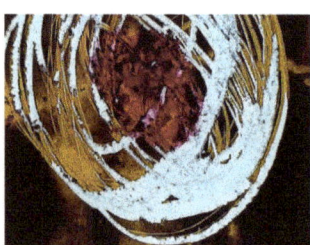
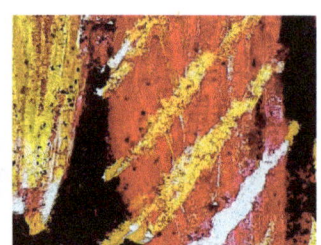

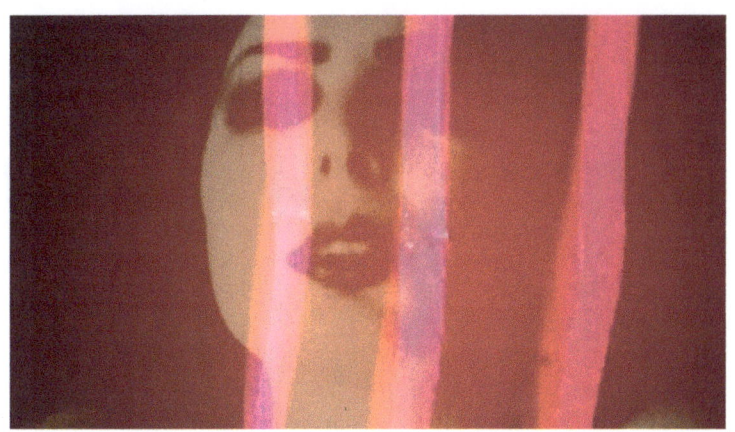

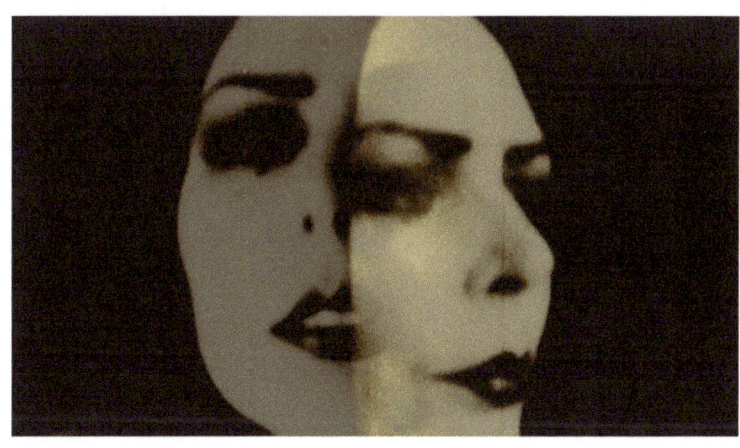

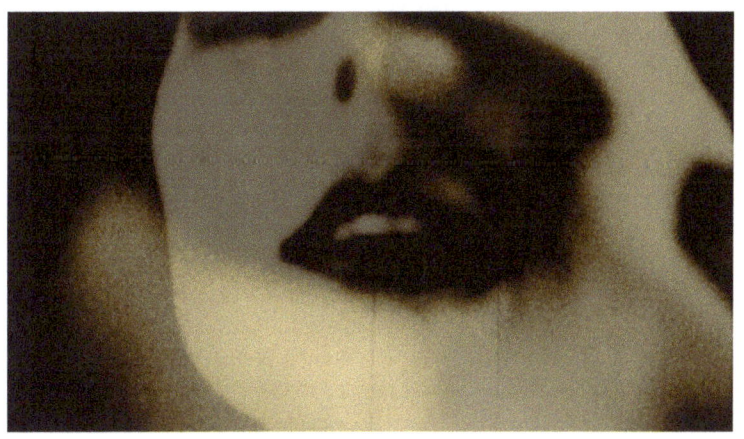

ssssensory exploratic

We love to have all these different options for Super 8 filmmaking and being able to handcraft film adds a whole other dimension.

What do you want your audience to walk away feeling after viewing this piece?

Sarahjane: The film was made within the Flow State, as we've said. When I was handcrafting each frame I lost time and whereabouts in order to create a kind of subjective or internal time-lapse of my life. I hope that some percentage of this is transferred to the viewer.

I hope that the viewer becomes immersed, sent on a visual and emotional journey of colour / movement / sensory exploration, and that the images somehow allow her to enter her own Flow State: a world of absolutely nothing but the immersion before her; to block out the world around her in that moment and allow herself to traverse the new and bold celluloid world before her. To lose track of space / time and moment. Lose self-consciousness and self-conscience and flow with the images into an experience of the unknown.

Any other film projects on the horizon?

Sarahjane & Roger: Well, one project we're excited about is getting the chance to handcraft and re-edit some analogue found film we've acquired.

We have a large reel of 16mm Home Movie footage shot in Sicily in the 1960s, which we bought on eBay. We've still not looked at any of this. As a starting point, we'll use the Light Box and jeweler's eye to check out some of the frames, to get an idea of what we're working with. We'll decide at that point whether we want to dive straight into handcrafting and manipulating the film, or to first get an HD digital scan of the un-treated footage.

We also have a big box of Super 8 film shot and processed in the 1970s or '80s which was donated to us along with a Braun Nizo camera and lots of other great stuff by a guy called Andy Swales. Andy was involved in an amateur analogue filmmaking club decades ago so we're intrigued to find out what's in those cartridges. We'll start off by creating

digital copies using our Winait telecine machine. We can send Andy copies of those in case he wants to look back through them and then we can get on with some handcrafting.

Our 16mm and 8mm Found Footage Experiments will result in more new releases as part of our Handcrafted Film Series, which began with "Flow State".

We're also working on some publishing projects, including a book using stills from "Flow State".

Another upcoming project: last year we were commissioned to create work for a programme set up by Glasgow University called Imprints of the New Modernist Editing. This was supposed to result in an exhibition in July at Shandy Hall in Yorkshire, one-time home of the 18th Century novelist, Laurence Sterne. Obviously, because of the Covid-19 crisis, this has been postponed till at least 2021. We're working on an interdisciplinary artwork for this - involving film, music, writing, stills and sculptural works - inspired by the final poem by the 19th Century French Symbolist poet, Stéphane Mallarmé. We're really excited to do this one and have already put a lot of work into the photography and the words but the whole project has had to be put on the back-burner for now. Once we get a few other things out the way we're going to get stuck right into working on the film elements: probably a mix of analogue, digital and handcrafted. What we're aiming towards is producing the exhibition / installation at Shandy Hall, and other venues, with all the different elements melded together to create one immersive experience for visitors. At the same time we also want to expand the project by producing a stand-alone film, a book and a soundtrack CD, so that the work can be approached from different angles - offering the viewer / reader / listener a distinct experience - but with each of these formats absolutely tied together thematically and stylistically. It's an ambitious project but our ideas for it are strong and so is our enthusiasm.

Anything else to add?

Sarahjane & Roger: Here are some ways Analog Cookbook's readers can check out our work. ->

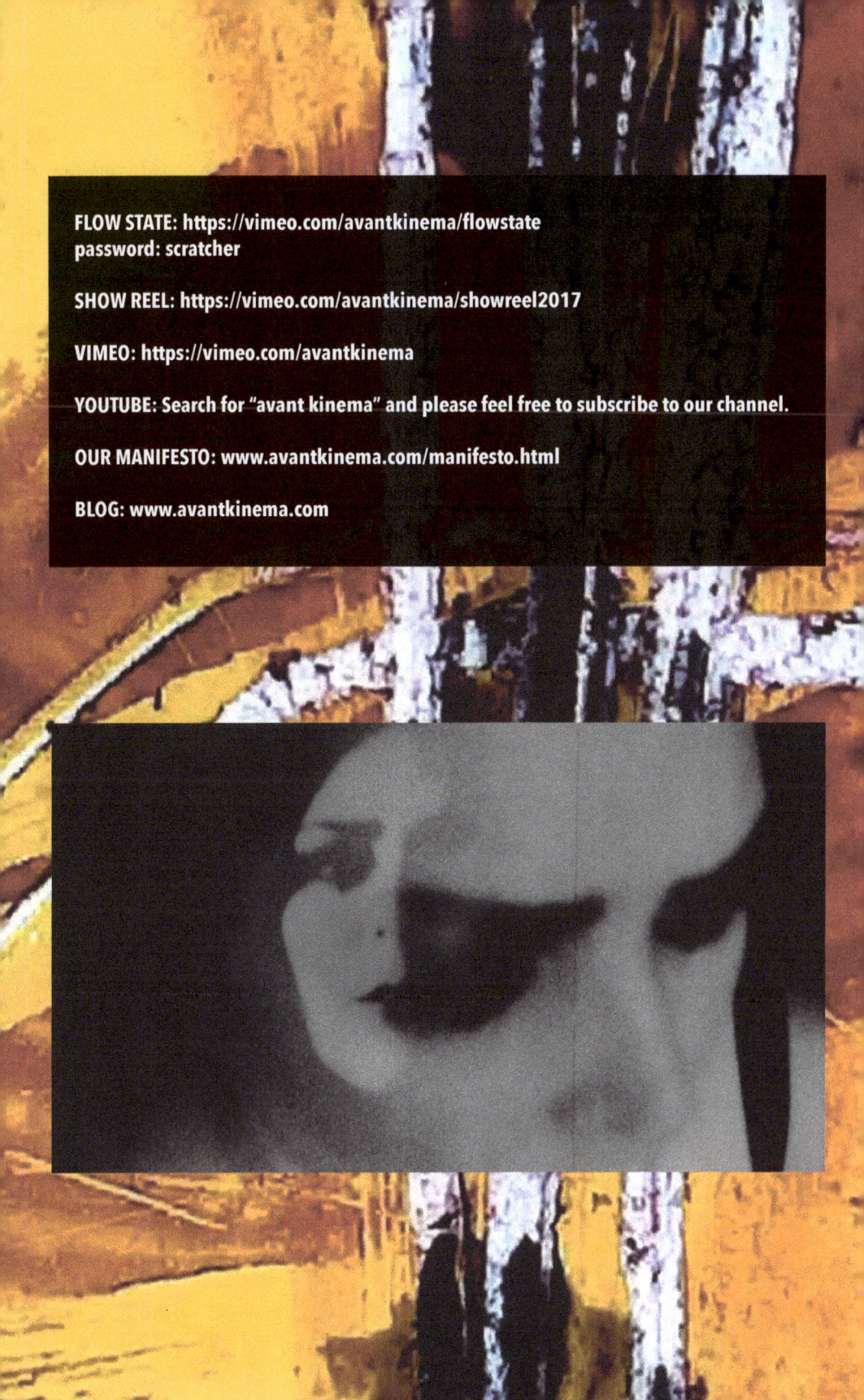

FLOW STATE: https://vimeo.com/avantkinema/flowstate
password: scratcher

SHOW REEL: https://vimeo.com/avantkinema/showreel2017

VIMEO: https://vimeo.com/avantkinema

YOUTUBE: Search for "avant kinema" and please feel free to subscribe to our channel.

OUR MANIFESTO: www.avantkinema.com/manifesto.html

BLOG: www.avantkinema.com

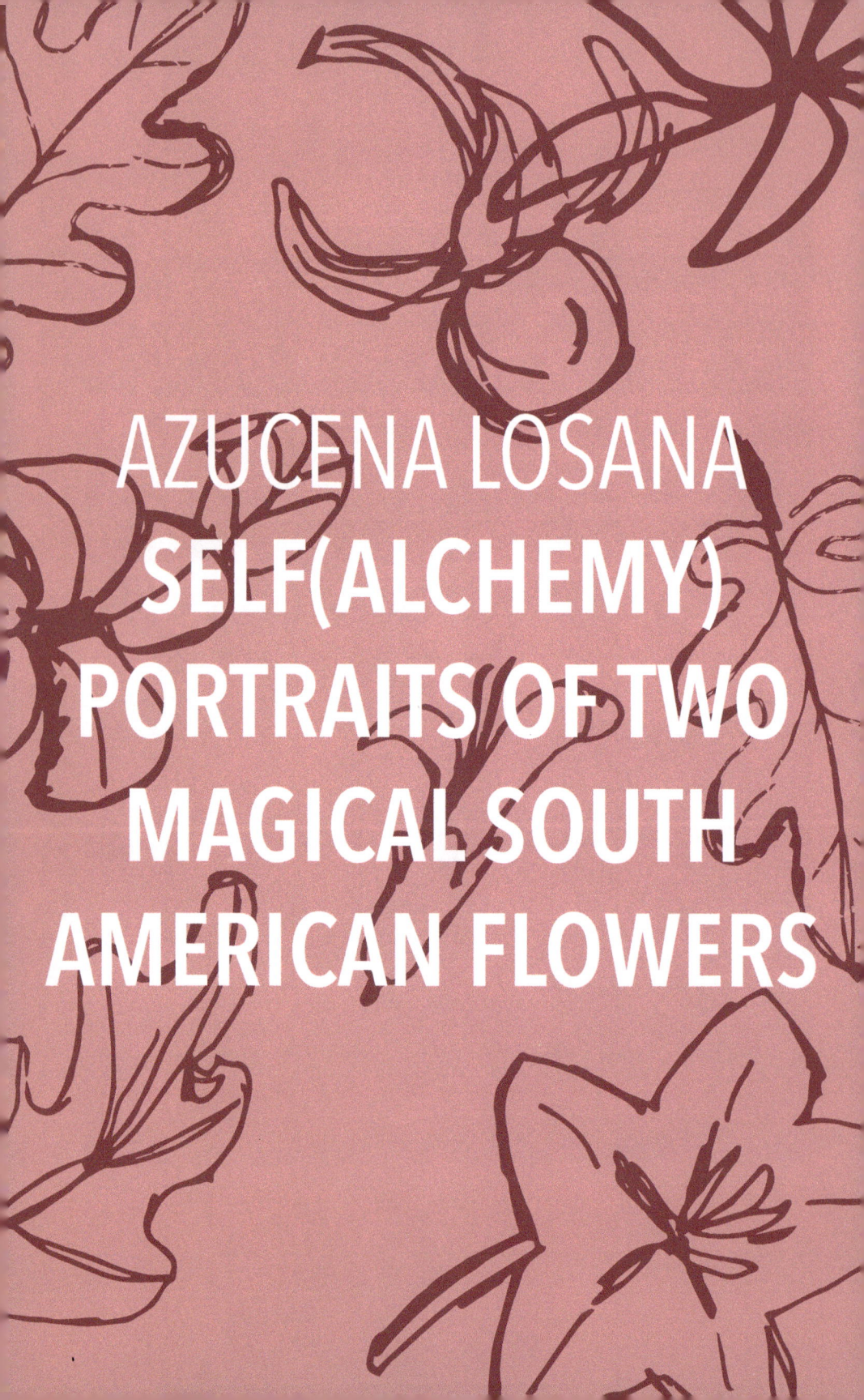

AZUCENA LOSANA
SELF(ALCHEMY) PORTRAITS OF TWO MAGICAL SOUTH AMERICAN FLOWERS

I worked for 5 years as a laboratorist on a mythical film lab in Buenos Aires specialized in developing black and white super 8 film. I learned how to deal with chemical processes and always wanted to figure out a way to develop my own films being more friendly with the environment and my own health! I've been inspired and assisted by the worldwide net friends working on alternative developing processes, such as Dagie Brundert in Germany and her "Yummy Soups", the experiments of Adrian Cousins in the UK, the DIY project The Sound We See of The Echo Park Film Center around the world and the investigation with local plants of Gral Treegan in Mexico.

On Roland Barthes' concepts of spectrum and punctum in photography, the photochemical process becomes an interdimensional portal that allows us to have our eyes touched by the same light that illuminated the subject of the portrait. In these short films our eyes are touched by the sunlight that illuminates these magical flowers and that fulfills them with alchemy powers through the photosynthesis. These flowers traditionally used as medicine and now are the active developer of their own image. I chose two endemic species very easy to find in most major cities in South America where most of the flowers are no longer used but as an ornament.

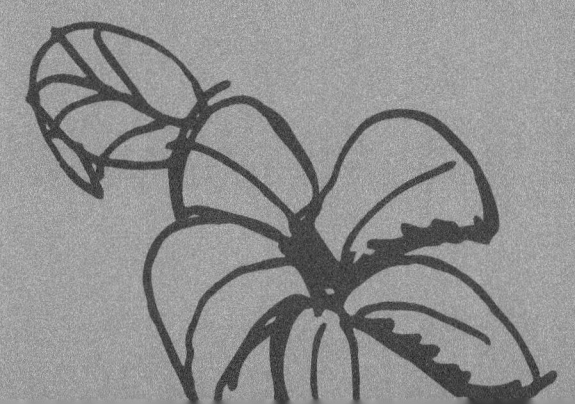

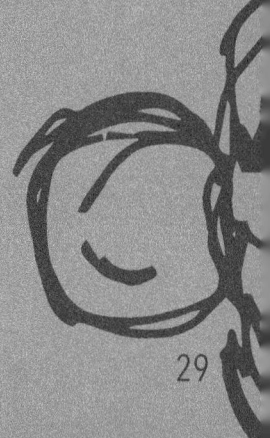

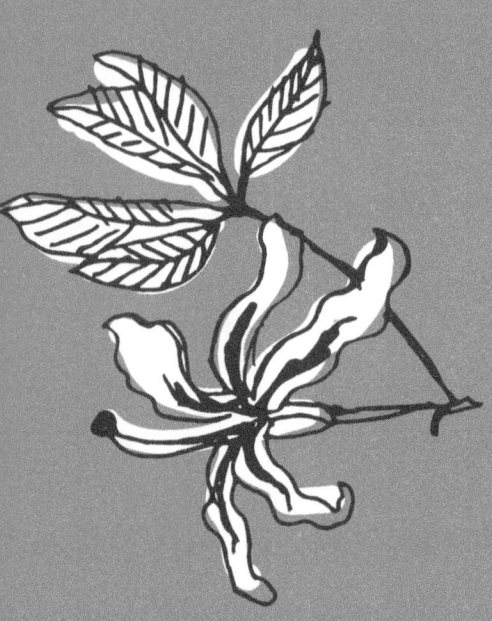

PALO BORRACHO (CEIBA SPECIOSA)

Common Names:
Algodonero, árbol botella, árbol de la lana, árbol de la seda, Chorisia, Palo Barrigudo, Paina de seda, Palo Rosado and Yucán (Spanish), Samu'ú o Mandiyu-ra (guaraní),
Copadalick (Qom/Toba) Chemlhokw (Wichi) Bottle tree (English) barriguda o painera (Brazilian
Portuguese).

This South American tree blooms during the summer and fall in almost all the great squares and
avenues of Buenos Aires. Its trunk is thorny and has a tummy to store water during droughts.
The flowers can be pink or white and are rich in the revealing agent nectar of this recipe.
The fruits are filled with cotton that protects the seeds, from which a vegetable oil is extracted
used as a supplement in some varieties of ayahuasca.
The native peoples of northern Argentina and Bolivia take the infusion of their flowers, thorns and leaves for joint pain, the regulation of the
female menstrual cycle and to cure inflammation of the urinary tract.

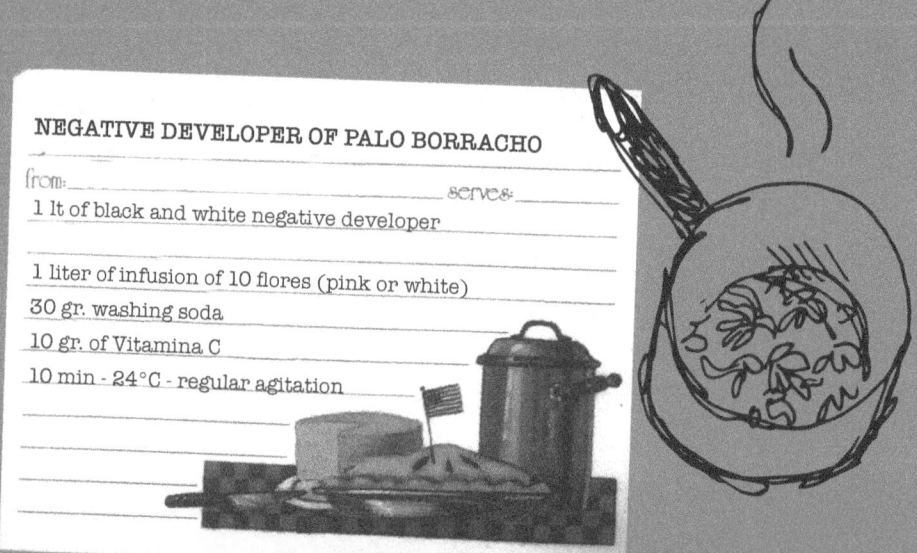

NEGATIVE DEVELOPER OF PALO BORRACHO

from:_____ serves:_____

1 lt of black and white negative developer

1 liter of infusion of 10 flores (pink or white)

30 gr. washing soda

10 gr. of Vitamina C

10 min - 24°C - regular agitation

TUTIA / ESPINA COLORADA (SOLANUM SISYMBRIFOLIUM)

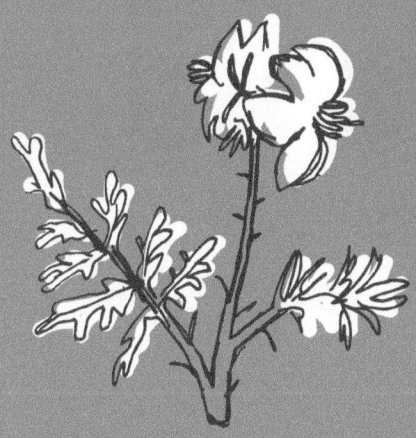

Common names:
Tútia, Revientacaballos, Espina colorada, Tomate del campo or Tomatillo (Spanish), Ñuati Pytá
(guaraní) Sikallu Warraqu (quechua), Llalli wangu (kallawaya), mamuel mapú lawuén (araucano),
neiák laaité (toba), Litchi Tomato (English).

This native South American weed is as aggressive as miraculous. It defends very well against
mammals with spines on its leaves, flowers and stem. The root and the leaves are used for liver,
intestinal and rheumatic diseases and as an anti-inflammatory. The fruits are edible and rich in
carotenes and lycopene (which in addition to giving it the red color is a great blood cleanser).
Like the entire Solanum family, is rich in solasodine, an alkaline that protects it from herbivores
and acts as a natural pesticide in potato plantations. Possibly also as the active developer in this
recipe.

NEGATIVE DEVELOPER OF TUTIA

from:_____ serves:_____

1 lt of black and white negative developer

1 liter of infusión of 30 gr. of leaves (preferably dry),
fresh flowers and/or ripe fruits (they must be bright red)

25 gr. of washing soda

10 gr. of ascorbic acid

10 - 15 min - 24°C - regular agitation

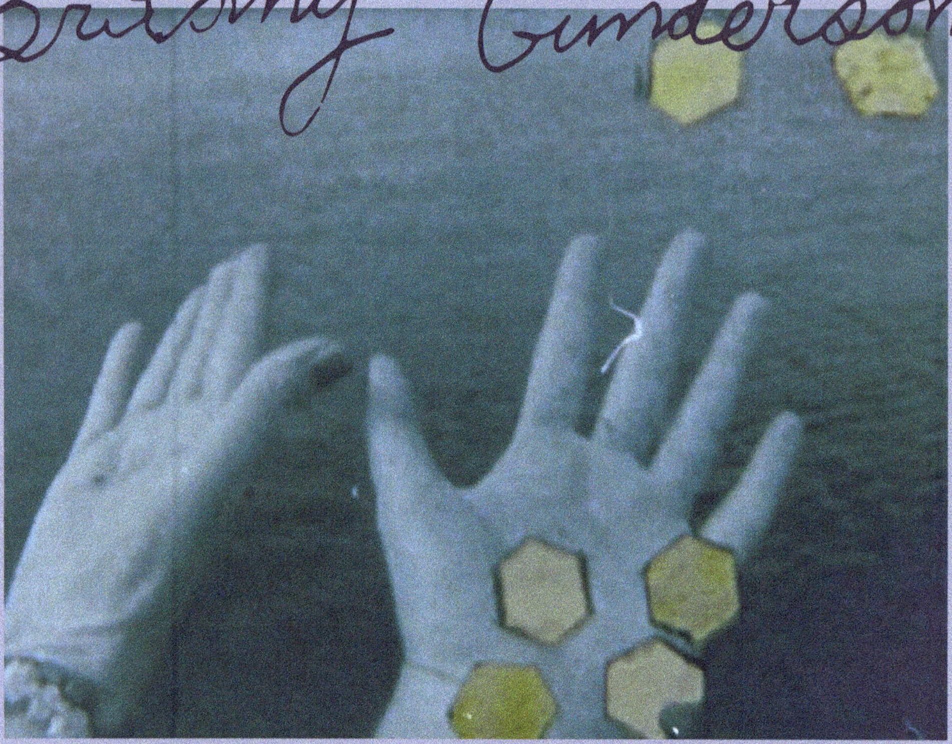

Britany Gunderson

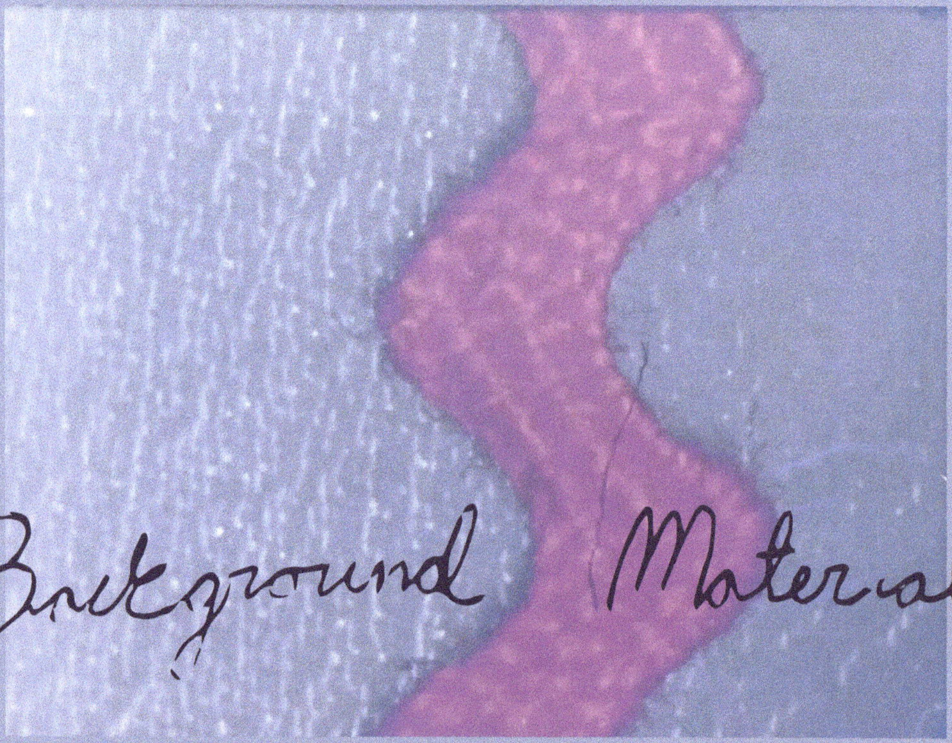

Background Material

TELL US ABOUT YOUR PROCESS WITH BACKGROUND MATERIAL.

I knew I wanted to make a film that revolved around the relationship I had with my mom, so I started to gather images and materials that reminded me of her or memories with her. I thought a lot about the idea of material memory, so I decided to shoot on 16mm film so I could engage with it a little more tactilely, and also planned to finish on film. I used an optical printer to front-light the physical objects on the film that I had glued and taped to the surface. Many of the fabrics and textiles featured were my mom's or my grandma's, like the big pink quilted blanket, and I had been collecting a lot of the material for years. So it really turned into a collection of moments, punctuated with a few real moments with my mom, past and present.

There's a moment in the film where thread is run through the film stock. This seems similar to your film Lining that was featured in Analog Cookbook Issue 2 what attracts you to this process?
It's definitely an interesting process, one that I tend to love and hate. I love the idea of being able to see physical objects on top of filmed images, animating those objects and bringing something stationary into the moving world. It's almost scientific, like the optical printer functions as a microscope and you can see all of the fuzz and dust and individual strands of thread, it's one of my favorite parts about the process. But it also adds an element of the uncontrollable, making it difficult to work with and not entirely knowing what the results will be. And it made sense in the context of my film, as a way to intervene with the image and showcase materials up close, revealing the textures. It let's two images live simultaneously.

What other materials did you apply directly to the film stock?
I used Rickrack trim (thread), glitter, and at one point a laser printed outline over found footage.

What do you hope your audience walks away feeling from this piece?
I guess it's kind of heavy, or maybe quietly heavy, and also personal. So I hope that it could serve as a connection to people who don't have a great relationship with their parents, or any relationship at all, and to feel understood or a little more recognized. I've always felt that the personal was off limits, afraid of sharing too much, but I've found that hearing other people's personal stories was really helpful in understanding my own. It's complicated and doesn't necessarily offer closure, but I don't think it needs to.

What film stocks did you use?
16mm Color Negative 50D and B&W Tri-X Reversal

Anything else to add?
I'm currently trying to get a print made for this film, so fingers crossed I'll have that soon!

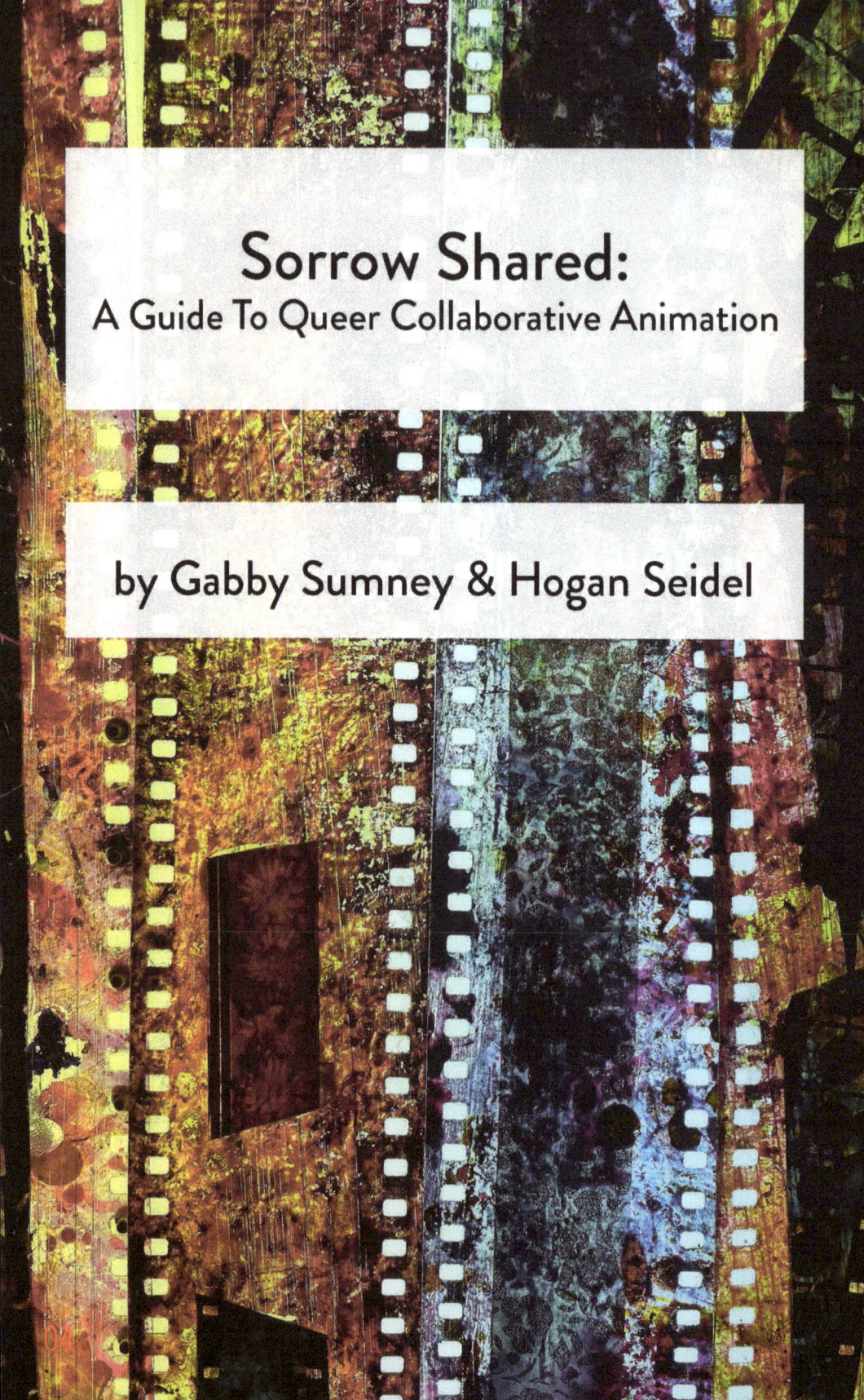

Sorrow Shared:
A Guide To Queer Collaborative Animation

by Gabby Sumney & Hogan Seidel

"Geteilte Freude ist doppelte Freude, geteilter Schmerz ist halber Schmerz."

In the fall of 2018, Hogan Seidel and Gabby Sumney decided to tackle a yearly collaboration called Sorrow Halved—from the German idiom "Geteilte Freude ist doppelte Freude, geteilter Schmerz ist halber Schmerz." or "A joy shared, is a joy doubled. A sorrow shared, is a sorrow halved." The two queer artists took a shine to the idiom as they considered ways to subvert traditional notions of authorship and the experimental canon in their practice and their teaching. The "sorrow" of singular creative genius that is often hailed in the experimental world felt counter to the lessons they were bringing to their students and to their approach to making queer art. Hogan & Gabby are both based in Boston, where they teach 16mm and experimental film. They both were interested in building pedagogical practices that incorporate collaborative modes of experimentation.

For one year, Gabby and Hogan took the same strip of 35mm clear leader and passed it back and forth every month. There were no restrictions on how to interact with the strip or limitations on materials. The artists were simply responding to each other through gestures. After the year was up, the artists collaboratively captured and edited the project on 16mm using contact printing and the optical printer. They plan to continue making a film each year indefinitely.

Ingredients Checklist:

☐ 2 or more Queers (for this recipe we used 2)

☐ 35mm acetate (200 ft) bought from Ebay

☐ Paints / Inks (calligraphy ink, acrylic, oil)

   [We personally love Higgins calligraphy ink]

☐ Tools to creatively place said paints and inks

   on film (paint brush, tooth brushes, rubber stamps,

   spray bottles)

☐ Things that also adhere to film (washi tape,

   glitter, nail polish)

☐ Glues (super and gorilla are our favorites)

☐ Other analog mediums to glue to the film

   (16mm, 35mm slide, super 8, reg 8)

☐ Household cleaning items [bleach, baking soda,

   salt, vinegar, steel wool]

☐ Transparency sticker paper (print what ya want

   and stick it to the film!)

Preparation

STEP 1

Queer #1 alters clear leader. They have 1 month to make something from nothing! Don't send progress photos to Queer #2. Queer #2 is supposed to respond in the moment. No peeking or preparation.

STEP 2

Queer #1 hands off film to Queer #2. Queer #2 can do whatever they want. They can add or destroy what has been given to them. Queer #1 is not allowed to get upset.

STEP 3

Lather, rinse, repeat. Continue steps number 1 and 2 until you are satisfied with your results. This can be made to be done in 1 hour or 1 year. We gave ourselves 1 year. Passing the film back and forth every month.

STEP 4

Converge! Watch the film together. This may be looking at it over a light table if it is too thick for a projector, or if you are like us and you dont have the money for a 35mm projector!

STEP 5

Devise your plan for post production! How do you want to print your film (or not)? We tested alternative methods of contact printing and optical printing. We ended up with a mixture of both.

STEP 6

Add titles, credits, and sound. We encourage you to use the same philosphy you did for making the film when you make the audio.

STEP 7

Decide when you want to start your next film! We are making one every year until we die.

Contact gfollettsumney@gmail.com & hoganseidel@gmail.com for any questions or clarification on our process.

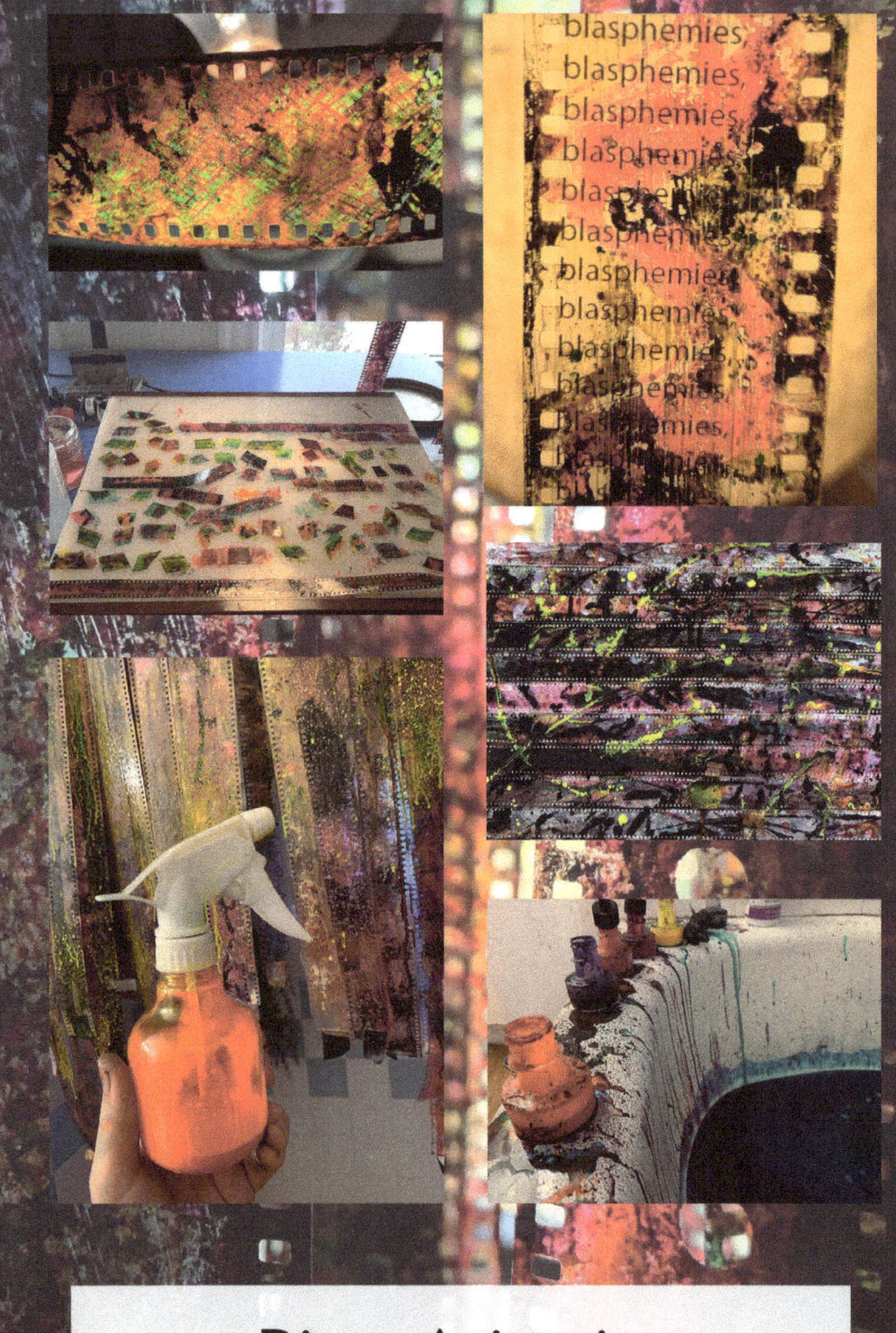

Direct Animation

Contact / Optical Printing

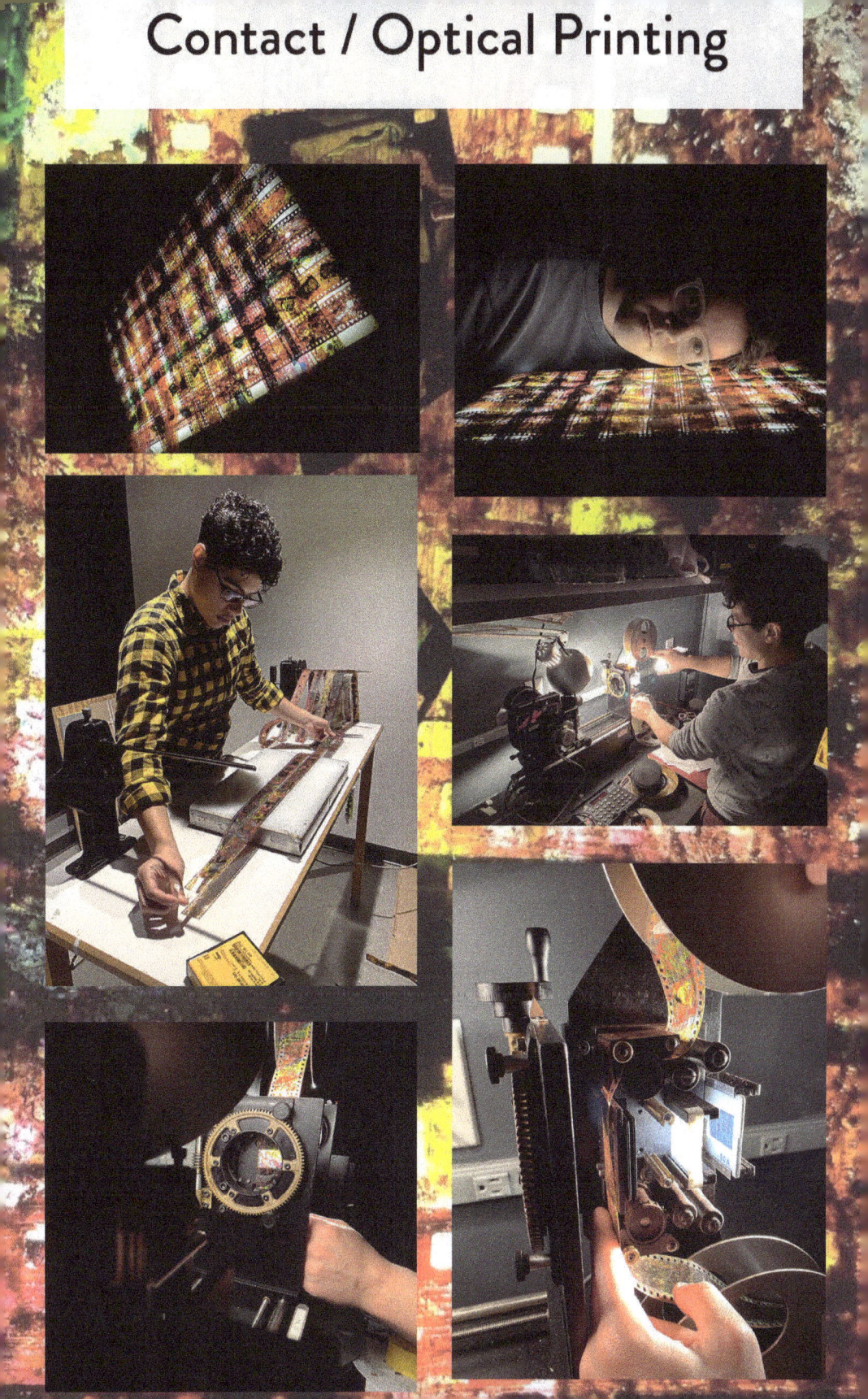

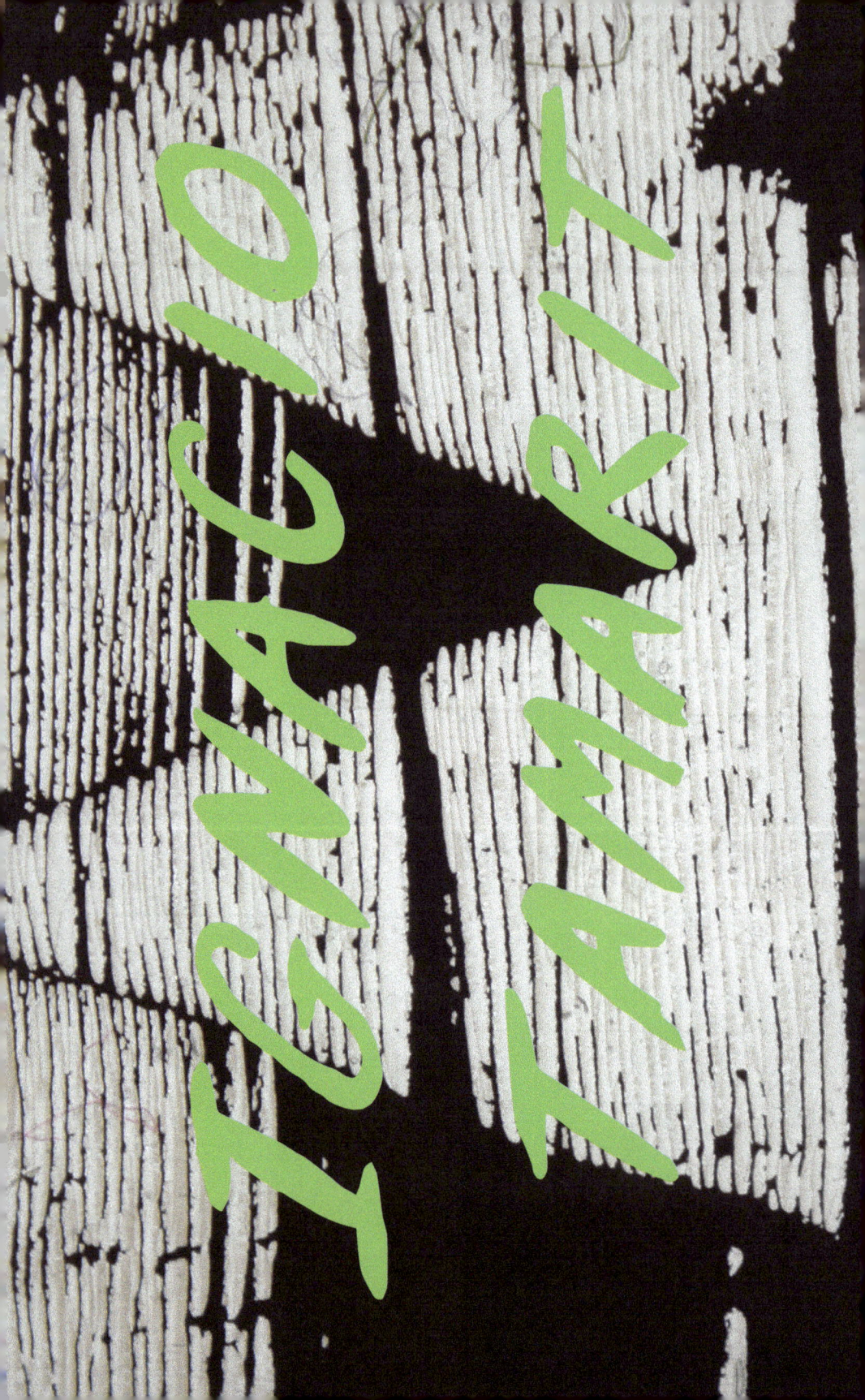

THE CREATIVE USE OF TAPES: HOW TO MAKE YOUR OWN BLACK LEADER FOR SMALL GAUGE FORMATS

Over the years I have experimented with various materials, tested techniques, and recycled materials, figuring out how to make cameraless films with what I have on hand. In Argentina and in a large part of Latin America it is very difficult to obtain cinematographic equipment and supplies to be able to work. This article is about how to generate black leader for small gauge formats such as super 8 and 16 mm.

In 2014 I made my first film without a camera on super 8, titled *Canción para Victoria*. It is a film that mixes live action footage on b & w film with abstract black and white imagery using VHS tape stuck on top of clear leader. At that time, I was looking for black leader to use as separators at the beginnings and ends of my films, but also, to use as inserts to generate spaced moments in movies. Since there are no stores that sell such supplies in the region, one has to figure out how to get, or achieve, black leader on their own.

I knew that one possibility was to buy virgin Tri-X film at the only laboratory that sells film in Argentina, only to process it without exposing it and having as a result, black film with D-Max. Obviously, this was the most expensive way, and the least suitable for me, since I make movies without a camera because I have no money to shoot! So, that was not a good option. Another possibility was to look for the tails of home movies that have not been exposed, which when processed remain black. But this requires

being lucky as well as spending a lot of time watching home movies and cutting those parts. Another possibility was the use of black electrical tape, which is 100% opaque. However, this tape is quite dense, and when applied on top of the film the film becomes heavy and. I had tried painting with black ink using black markers on clear leader but these methods did not work either, as they left an aesthetic imprint of the textures from those materials. I wanted to have full black throughout the film strip. By clear leader I am referring to found footage that I have bleached, since once again, there is no way to acquire this type of supply fresh from a store here.

Back then, with my colleague Dante Litvak who played in our misshapen punk band Méjico, we bought a VHS camera to tape our rehearsals, gigs, and the music scene of the community in which we were involved. I started making many cassettes. It was with a loose reel of VHS, which I had pulled out of a tape by breaking it, that I realized this tape was very thin, and opaque enough to be used as black leader.

On the worktable I put clear leader, well fastened at both ends with paper tape. On top of that I applied double-sided tape. The key is to find a tape that has no texture in the glue and is as translucent as possible. There was an issue where the smallest width of tape I could find in art supply stores was 12mm, and the super 8 is 8mm wide, so there is 4mm to spare. Next, you adhere the tape tight to the edge of the sprocket holes without covering them at all, the rest of the tape will cover the film and you can ignore the excess for now. Once the double-sided tape is attached to the film stick a piece of VHS tape on top. With a spatula, or other firm edge,

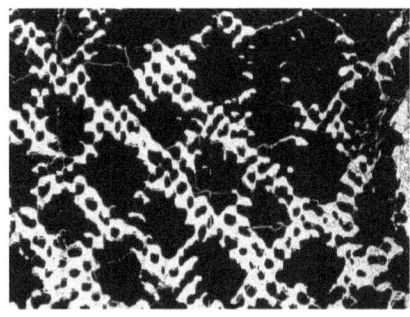

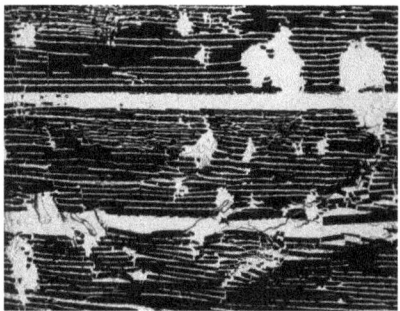

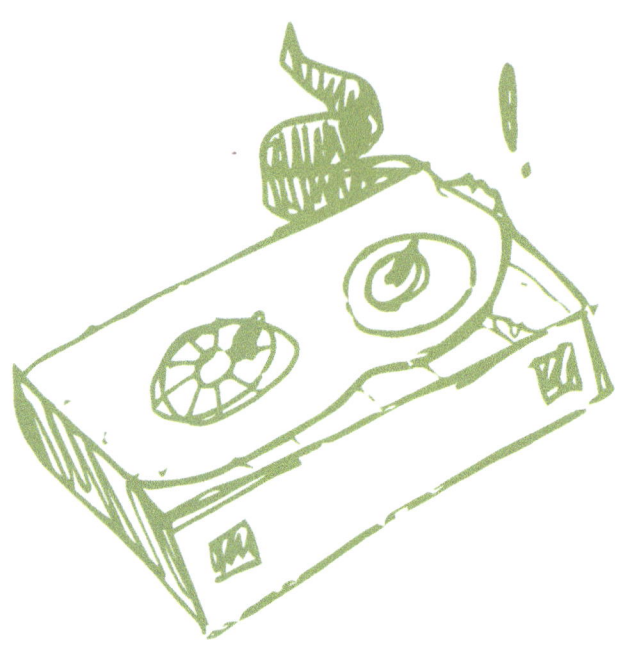

press along the tape so that it is well glued.
Now you have to turn the film, and with an X-Acto knife and ruler, trim the excess.

AND VOILA! BLACK LEADER!

When I made my film in 2014, I had accidentally stuck packing tape onto a strip of VHS tape that was on my desk. Tugging to remove it, the packing tape lifted some of the "skin" from the VHS, leaving behind incredible textures that I quickly decided to use as an aesthetic resource in the film. All the abstract images seen in the film were made based on the materiality of the VHS tape and this transfer technique.

A few years later, in 2018, I decided to make a completely abstract 16mm film, using solely the VHS tape as raw material, titled "In Film / On Video". I noticed that VHS tape is almost exactly the same width as the 16 mm, and that I could use it without having to trim the excess, as was necessary with the super 8.

I was very interested in the materiality of the VHS tape, a medium in which one cannot see the informational content, since it is pure black, magnetic tape - unlike a cinematographic film strip, where one can see images in the frames. Using the 16mm clear leader as a skeleton to support the magnetic tape provided a way to "see" the "informational content" of the magnetic tape as it was now able to be projected. Additionally, since the VHS tape occupies more space than the image area of the film, falling also into the sound area, the altered VHS tape generates a sound in the optical track. A mixture of film and video, two formats seemingly always at odds, which coexist here mutually.

In a time where purchasing film is expensive, and access is limited depending on your geographical location, it is a great moment to make cameraless films! The act of repurposing and recycling materials is integral to my practice. In the words of The Minutemen, *"WE JAM ECONO"*

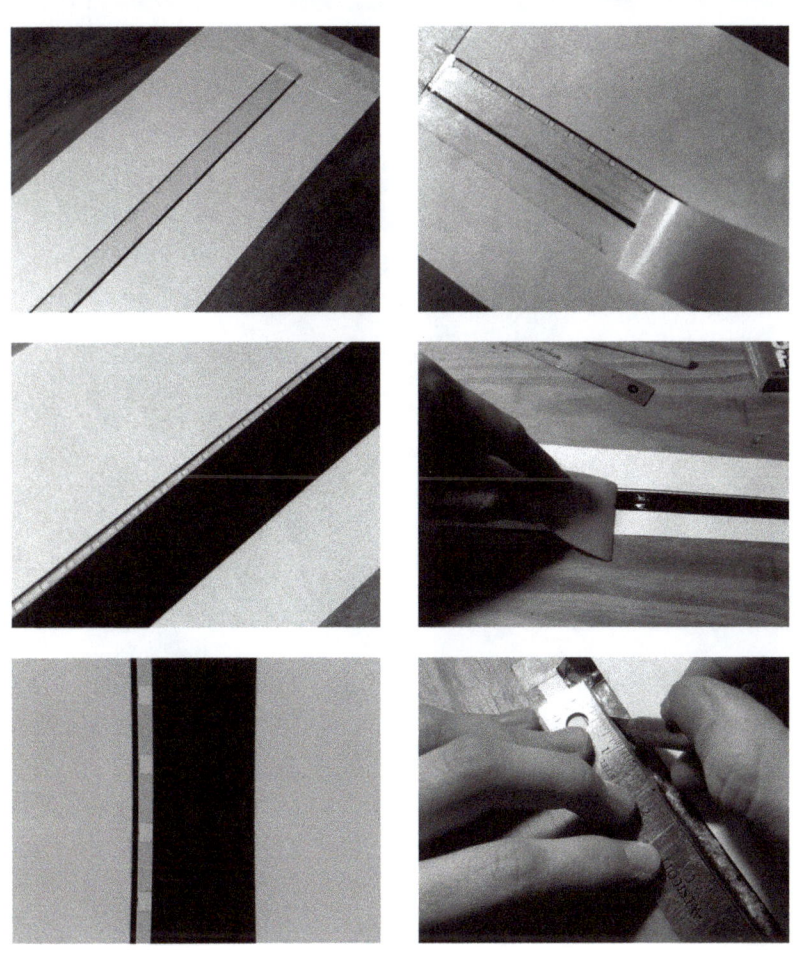

I WAS VERY INTERESTED
IN THE MATERIALITY OF
THE VHS TAPE, A MEDIUM
IN WHICH ONE CANNOT
SEE INFORMATIONAL CONTENT

Iuan Salamao &

Ata Nayana Ferreira

44

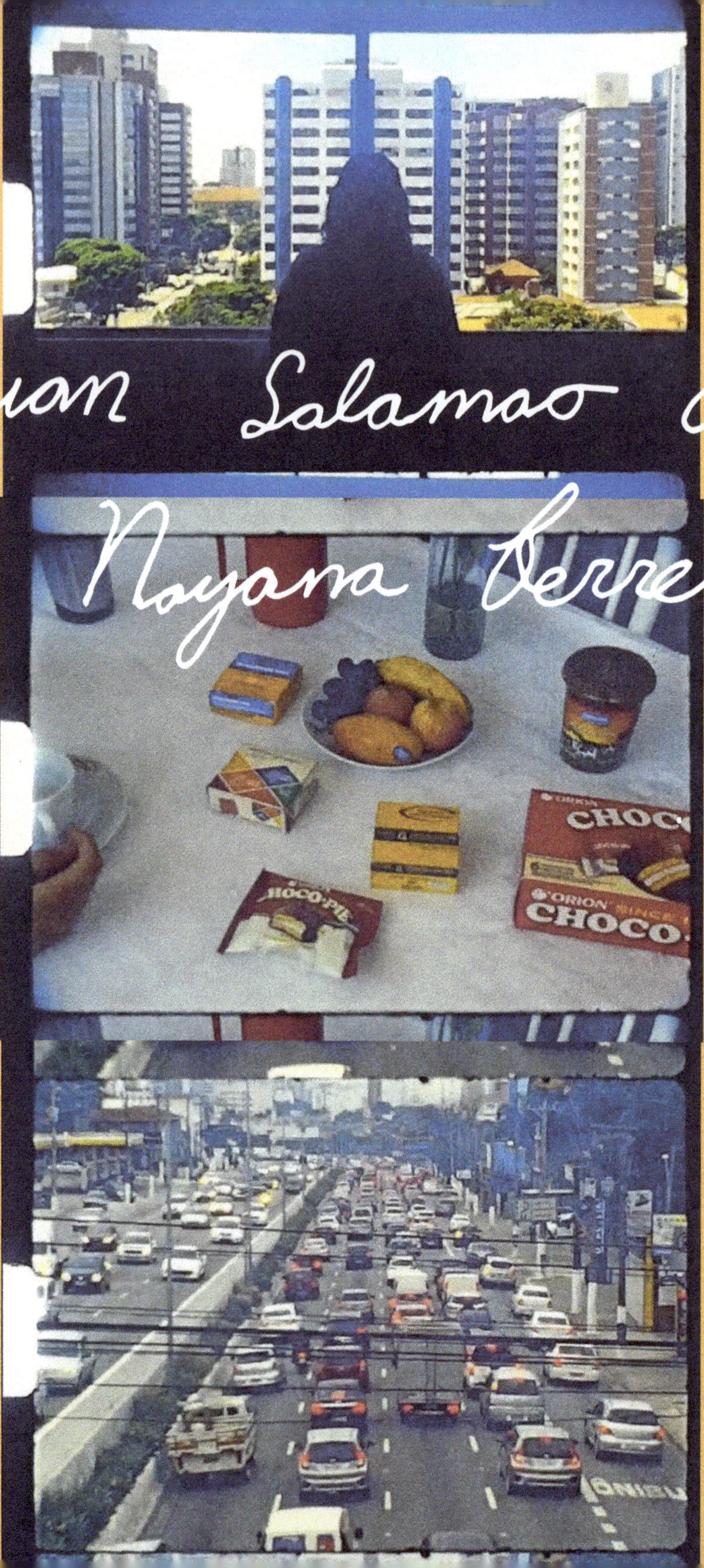

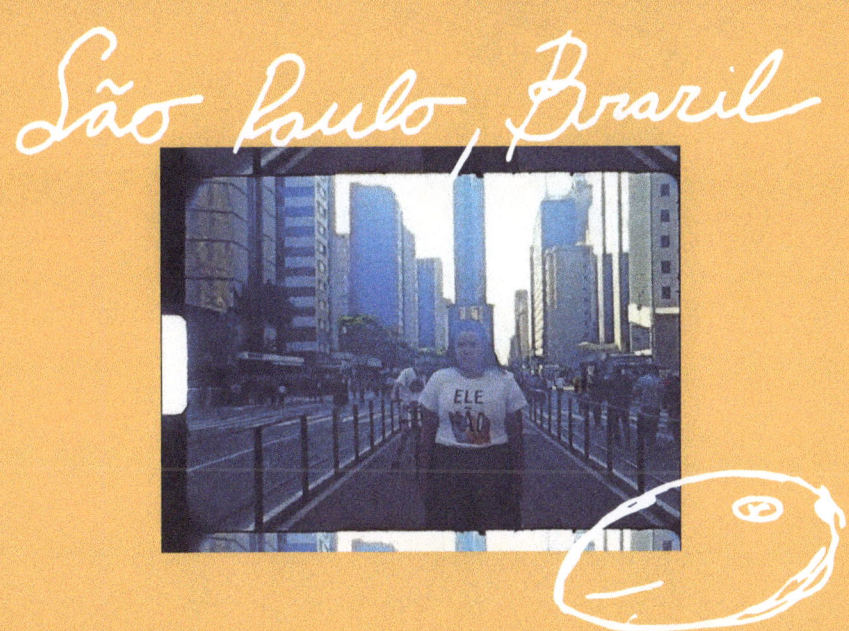

HOW WAS THE FILM DEVELOPED?

The film was made in São Paulo, Brazil in October 2018 when the elections for the new president were taking place.It was made from a color film Kodak 7285 development by E6 process. It was developed during workshop given by Distruktor from Berlin in Brazil. It was a very nice workshop because we connect some artists who wanted to develop color film. And belive, one of workshop day´s was the voting day! We feel welcomed during such a sad day.

You filmed this on the eve of the 2018 Brazilian presidential election. Why was it important to document this moment?
This was a historic moment in Brazil, it was important to note that in times of hatred, there was a love between others, that there are both sides in this election.

Throughout the film, we see both bustling city life and quiet domestic moments. What was the process behind this?
The film emerged from a course on developing color films. It was necessary to have color in the film, it was a couple who made the film so there was love,

the calm of their home, of their day, but there was chaos outside the city where a presidential election pulsed that would change the course of Brazil.

Why was it important to shoot this on super 8mm?
We used the Super 8 a lot as a way of recording our experiences. This was a historic moment, there were many TV recordings and we wanted to leave our record with the film we worked with,something to be watched here for 15, 20 years too.

What do you hope your audience walks away feeling after watching this piece?
We hope that the public will see this duality that in times of hatred, there is love. That we young people will not let the community get lost in the face of so much horror.

What's next for you?
We are still filming in Super 8, despite so many difficulties. Right now, we are making a film about the pandemic that is in everyone, looking from inside the house, but that can reflect in many families. Long live the Super 8, long live the cinema of Latin America. And may better days come for everyone.

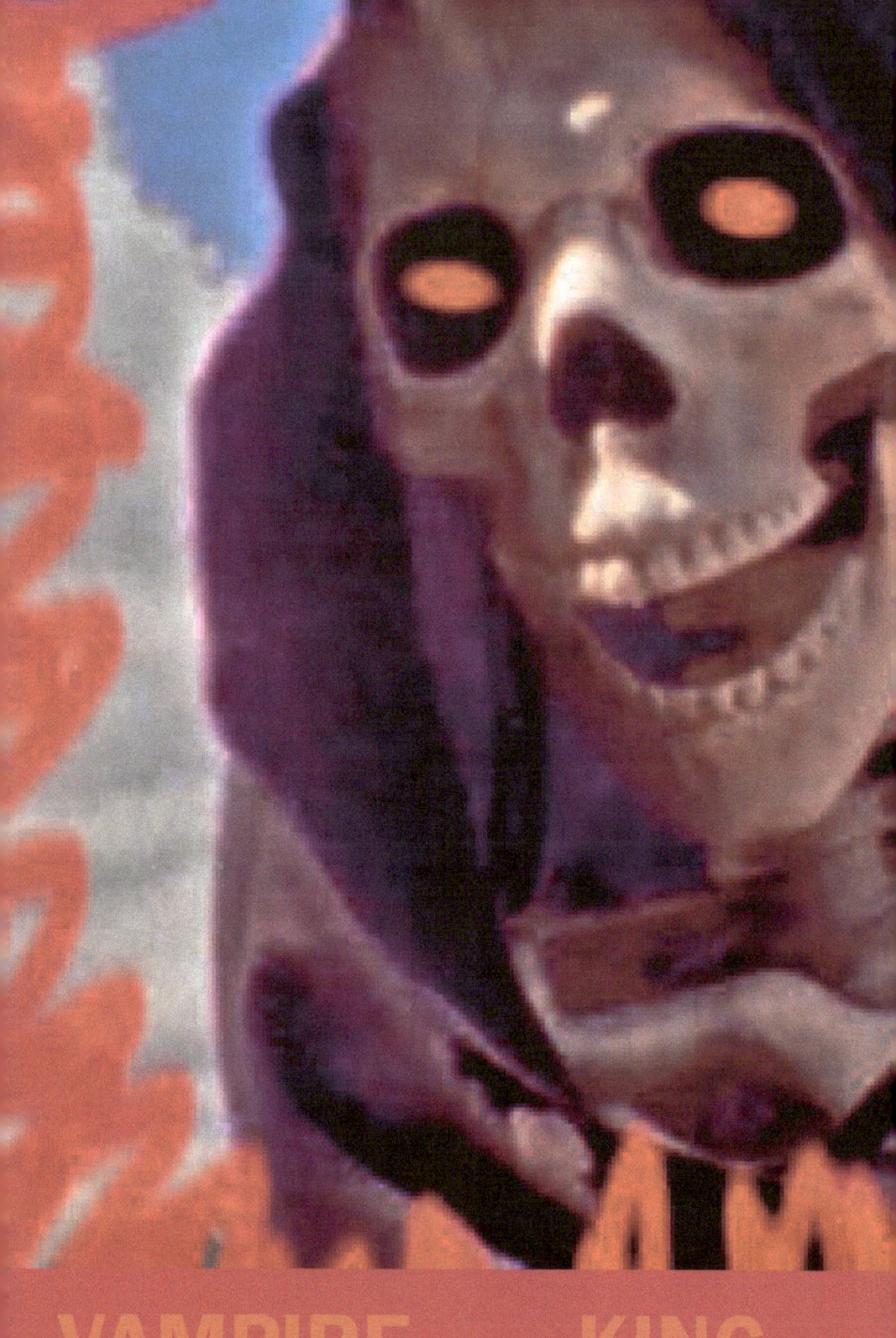

VAMPIRE   KING

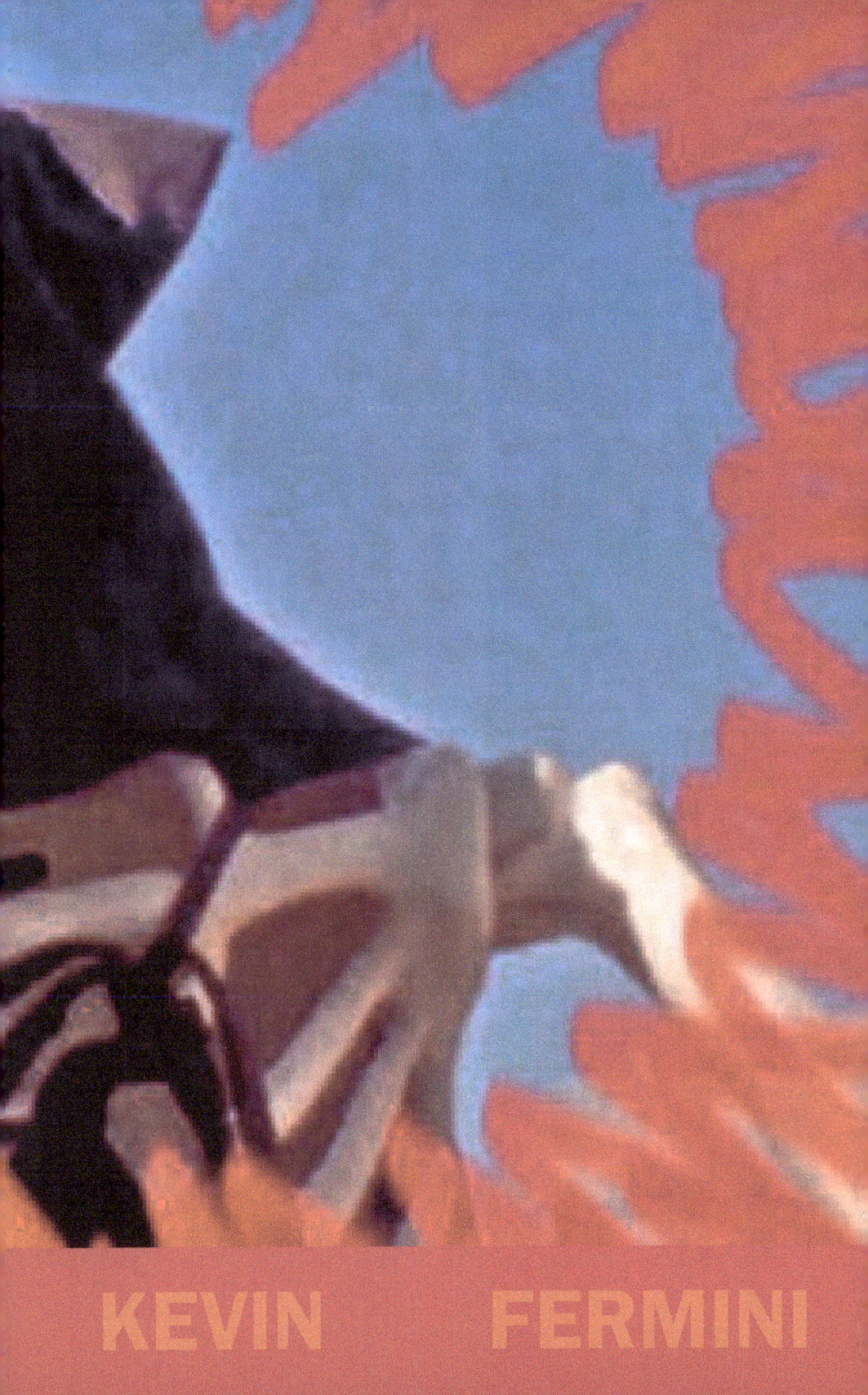

TELL US ABOUT YOUR PROCESS. HOW DID VIOLA VS. THE VAMPIRE KING COME TO BE?

Viola was very much a culmination of all my cinematic interests up until the point I made it. I have a very soft spot in my heart for b-movies, not only for the fact that I've inherently loved monsters and weird fantasy since I was a kid -- but also because so many b-movies end up being documents of the people that made them, too. When you dig back through the films of directors like Herschell Gordon Lewis or Ed Wood, you naturally start to pick apart some of the amateur camera moves, the seams on the monster costumes, stuff like that. But truthfully, I find those quirks incredibly endearing and inspiring, to the point where I feel as if I'm learning more about filmmaking each time I watch them.

That love sort of culminated when I dug up an issue of this old filmmaking magazine called Cinemagic. If there's one piece of wisdom I want to impart on analog filmmakers, it's to go dig up some issues of Cinemagic and have a wild afternoon. The magazine was founded by Don Dohler in 1972. Dohler is a beloved DIY b-movie director in his own right (check out Night Beast or Alien Factor), and he teaches you everything from how to build miniatures in your garage, to using double exposures to paint UFOs into your shots, to how to make prosthetic limbs and build wireframe monsters. There's even a Letters To The Editor section in which people would write to Don about the DIY films they were making, many of which I've been able to look up and find hidden in the dark recesses of YouTube or Vimeo. It's truly a wondrous and playful publication for anyone interested in analog filmmaking.

Needless to say, the films I had absorbed and the secrets Cinemagic was teaching me brought me to a point where I knew the film had to be made. The film ultimately is just stockpiled with monster makeup, stop motion, miniature wax animation, direct animation, prosthetic limbs and blood cannons -- but it's all done with the intent to charm the audience and invite them into the filmmaking process in a playful, inspiring way.

What film stocks did you use?
Honestly, pretty straightforward stuff. Kodak Vision3 50D color negative for the exteriors, and 250T for the interiors -- both in 50ft cartridges.

What camera did you use to shoot this film?
My good ol' Canon 518 AutoZoom. I picked it up off of eBay a few years ago for something like $35, from someone who couldn't tell me if it worked or not. Turns out I got super lucky, that camera worked like a dream and has been by my side on numerous projects since.

For anyone looking for a Super 8 camera to start out on, I can't recommend it enough. Between its ability to shoot at 18, 24 or 36fps; being able to do single frame animation; and a fast, snappy zoom lens that opens up to f/1.8 -- it's really everything you need in one package!

I'm glad to say I got nearly 5 years of use out of that camera, but regretfully the motor seems to have stopped working as of a few months ago. If anyone knows someone who can open the thing up and take a look -- let me know!

Why was it important to share a fantasy horror film on Super 8?
That's a really great question! There were honestly a lot of motivating factors that led to the decision to shoot the film on Super 8.

At the end of the day I think Viola is simply escapist entertainment. Part of my goal in making it was to create something that felt totally separate from our current reality, in more ways than one.

The great thing about Super 8 (and working with film as a whole), is that it inherently has a reflexive and nostalgic quality to it. The wonderful imperfections of film draw the viewer's attention to the fact that they're watching something physically different from a digital film, which in turn makes it feel like something out of our time. With that in mind, my hope was that Viola could

C H I L D H O O D
FEVER   DREAM

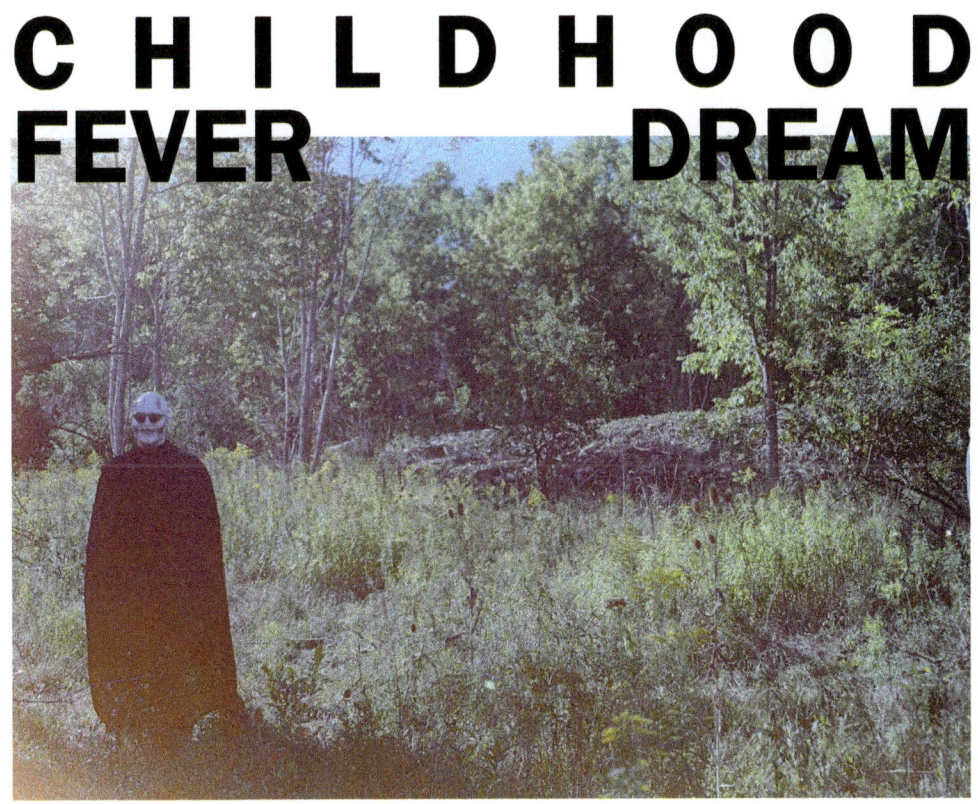

feel equally like some sort of old, demented children's fantasy film that had been dug out of a vault somewhere; or that it could feel simply like a childhood fever dream -- a story you acted out with your friends playing in the woods one afternoon. What's fun too is that the latter sort of became true as we made the film, it really was just a bunch of us out in the woods in costumes making this thing, trying out camera techniques and crude special effects. I think the innocent fun of that manages to come through in the piece a little bit, and I'm very happy about that.

Who are some of your artistic inspirations?

On a filmmaking level, my world changed when I discovered Nobuhiko Obayashi. He's best known here in the states for directing House (1977) -- a film incredibly near and dear to my heart. His filmmaking beyond House is equally as wonderful, especially his early shorts. All of his films play with form in such a pure way, and breaking down the cinematic language he's more or less invented for himself is a joy. It's comedic, effective and highly inviting -- it makes you want to grab a camera and go see what you can make! I also love and admire Shinya Tsukamoto, Seijun Suzuki, Wong Kar Wai, Lucio Fulci, Zia Anger and George Romero, and currently have been discovering Agnes Varda and loving what I've seen. Films that push style and emotion to the forefront are my favorites -- subtly has its place, but I find that I fall in love with films that are maximalist rather than minimalist.

B-movies -- especially the subgenre of shot-on-video films which I've recently been diving into, are also a huge inspiration because of how they often end up becoming documents of low-budget, passion driven filmmaking. Huge shout outs to the Polonia brothers and Damon Packard in this regard (his film Reflections of Evil is a necessary experience).

49

Beyond filmmaking, I'm constantly going back to the music of Frank Zappa, Herbie Hancock and Charles Mingus for inspiration. What unites those musicians, in my opinion, is that despite the intense craft and theory that goes into their work -- their music comes out feeling completely spontaneous. In filmmaking I think that's one of the greatest things you can achieve -- making even your most carefully planned and rehearsed setups look natural, as if they just emerged ordinarily out of the world you've created.

Do you have a favorite/go-to tool when working with film?

When I was in college, I was lucky enough to edit a film I shot on 16mm on a flatbed Steenbeck editor, and I feel like it forever changed my approach to editing.

I'm not going to encourage anyone to go out and get themselves a Steenbeck by any means -- but I do think it's important to emphasize the physical nature of working with film and how it affects a filmmaker's workflow.

Lately I've seen tons and tons of digital products online which advertise film overlays, film texture or film grain you can overlay onto your digital footage. While I'm not opposed to those kinds of things by any means -- I honestly feel like shooting film like shooting film is like another medium of filmmaking, much like watercolor is a different medium of painting than pastel. No matter how convincing the overlay, you'll never capture the same image on a digital camera that you will staring down the viewfinder of a dusty Super 8 camera, keeping constant attention to your footage counter and framing your shots through a worn mechanical lens.

So I'll just say -- get involved, get direct, get physical with it (by the way I hope this answer works, haha. If you want me to focus more on something specific I can do that).

What's next for you?

Earlier this year I finished up another Super 8 short called DEATH WALKS ON NITRATE. It's a giallo-inspired, psychedelic horror film about a photographer who crosses paths with a mysterious old woman. It's been playing a bunch of virtual film festivals, and hopefully I'll be able to see it play in a theater with an audience sooner than later, as that's what I really made it for. But it's made good momentum so far; it'll be playing at Arrow Video's Frightfest this year which is a big honor -- and the jazzy, psychedelic soundtrack was even picked up for a vinyl release that'll be coming out this fall!

Beyond that, I shoot and direct music videos and commercials here in Atlanta so I've always got something going on. If you wanna follow me @ kevinfermini on Instagram you can check that stuff out!

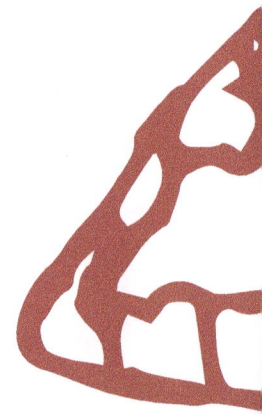

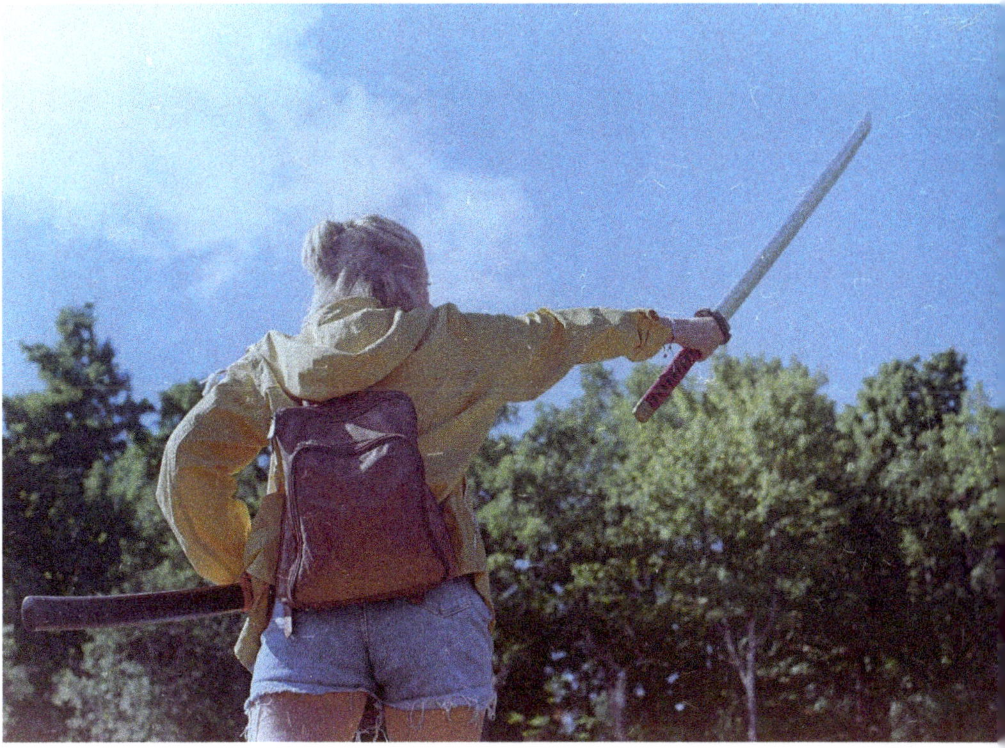

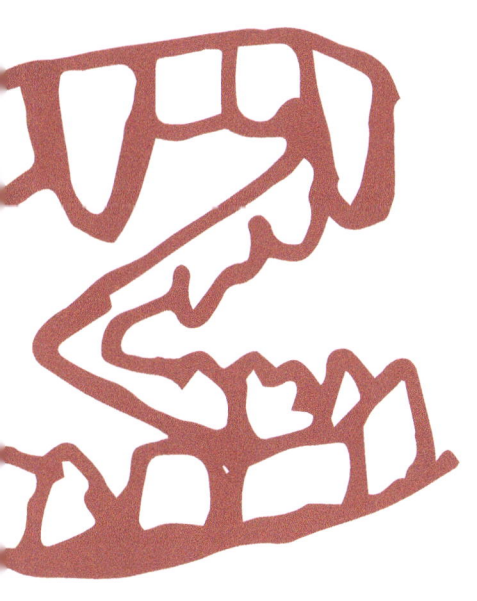

LAUREN
HENSCHEL

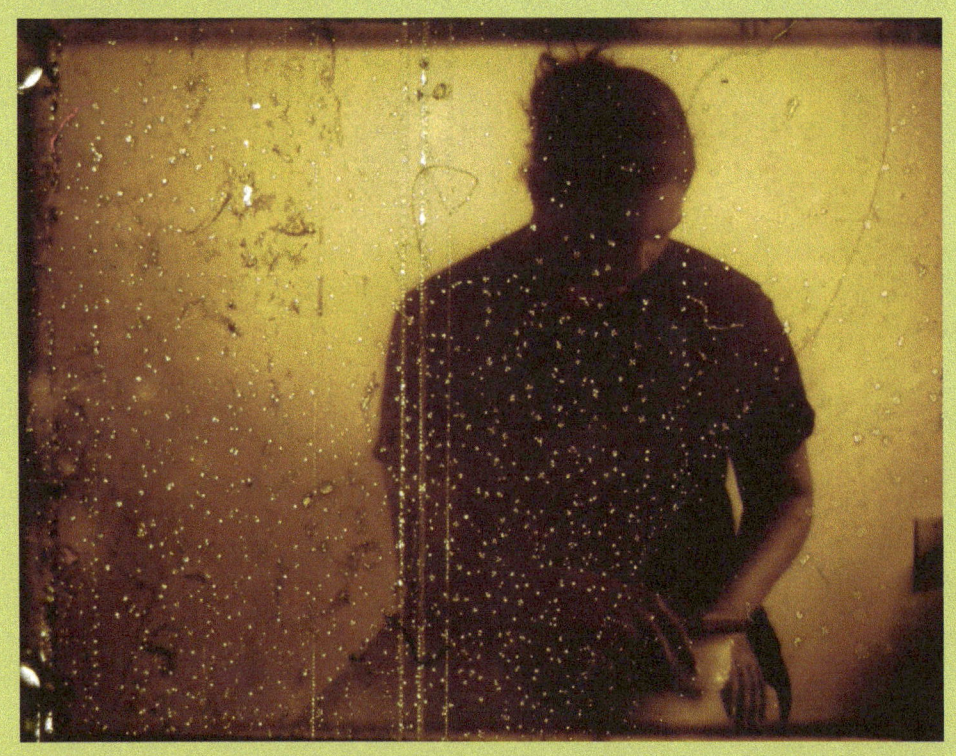

TELL US A BIT ABOUT YOUR BACKGROUND. WHEN DID YOU FIRST START WORKING WITH FILM?

When I was 15, I was on track to play college basketball and then all of a sudden it felt like cement had been poured into all the crevices of my body. I was diagnosed with Psoriatic Arthritis, an autoimmune disease, and I turned to my moms camera as an outlet. I spent a lot of time in college working with digital moving image, but it never totally felt right. I knew I had a story to tell about my experience, but it wasn't until I picked up a Bolex for the first time at the beginning of my MFA at Duke in 2018 that I knew I found a way to communicate artistically about my body.

What film stock did you use for Infusion No. 1? Do you have a favorite/go-to film stock?

I have only ever worked with 3378 except for a few urges to shoot a roll or two on color film. My whole process is centered around thinking about film as an extension of my body, or as its own body. 3378 is really cheap, easy to hand-process and allows me to process my film in medication, bodily fluids, or whatever else I can get my hands on without worrying about perfection while I'm experimenting. Although you need a TON of light while working with 3378, I find that to be the only limiting factor and feel a freedom with this stock that I've never felt in any artistic process.

Tell us about portraying chronic illness on film.

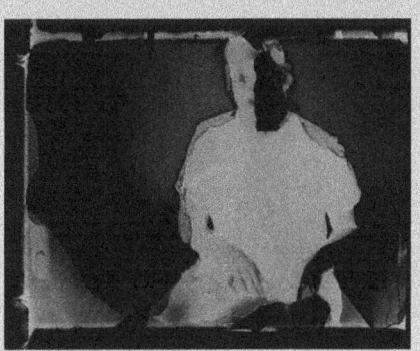

When I began my MFA at Duke two years ago, I knew I wanted to document my experience with chronic illness, but the illnesses I deal with on a daily basis are largely invisible. It then became a question of how I could translate my experience. There are so many chronic illnesses and no one's experience will be exactly like someone else's experience so I think the work became about asking others to re-encounter their own awareness of inhabiting a body.

The recent spread of COVID has forced people everywhere to feel some degree of fear and disillusionment with how safe they feel in their bodies—something that the immunocompromised, and the greater community of people with disabilities, experience as a constant. Right now we are all struggling with the idea that we are residing in the temporary shelter of a body, of the impermanent and illusory concept of being well.

Which chemicals did you use to alter the film? How did you incorporate medicine into this process?

This film was captured on 3378 film stock and processed as reversal. It is on one roll of film and was performed as a single take of my injection. I then spliced the film in the dark based on where I thought different movements were happening and dumped different sections of the film into different chemicals. I intentionally wore black and filmed against a white wall because I knew the chemicals would destroy the densest part of the image first. After that, I was just dropping selections of the film in different buckets- toner, bleach, my injection, hydrogen peroxide, cough syrup, vitamins, bodily fluids, you name it! I wanted portions of the film to mimic what I put into my body to make it work. This was meant to be a test, but when I spliced the film back together and projected, what appeared on screen felt raw and true to my own experience. The film deteriorates and flares at the moment of injection, making visible this invisible ritual. I pretty much didn't change a thing after that one darkroom session.

There are times in the piece where the body disappears altogether or double exposure occur. Can you talk about these choices?

There is one section of the film that was added later. I made a contact print inside of the bolex of about 20 seconds of the film and instead of using light to make the print, I filmed myself looking back at the viewer through the footage of the injection. There is a gaze or a looked-at-ness that often occurs with bodies that aren't what the world deems "normal" and without getting into too much detail, I wanted this to be a moment in which I looked back at the viewer.

How do you feel about portraying personal moments on film?

There is so much beauty in the banal. My experience with illness is not extraordinary by any means, but I think there is something amazing that happens when someone just lays their experience out for you. It makes these big, scary things we keep inside

and fear like illness, genetics and shame more ordinary. By getting really specific and personal in my own work, I just hope others feel safe exploring their own body and experience.

Who are some of your artistic inspirations?

Leslie Jamison, Barbara Hammer, Carolyn Lazard, Sadie Benning, Naomi Uman, David Gatten, Steve Cossman .

What's next for you?

Right now I am adjunct teaching at Duke, making some new work and doing some research with the Gender, Sexuality and Feminism department.

INFUSION NO. 1 was one of the films projected in my MFA thesis installation, but the show never happened because of COVID, so I am still focussed on getting that work out into the world. The center of the installation is a giant room of live mushrooms, so we will see what state it is in once everything returns to a new normal.

Anything else to add?

Seek out film positive communities! MONO NO AWARE changed everything for me.

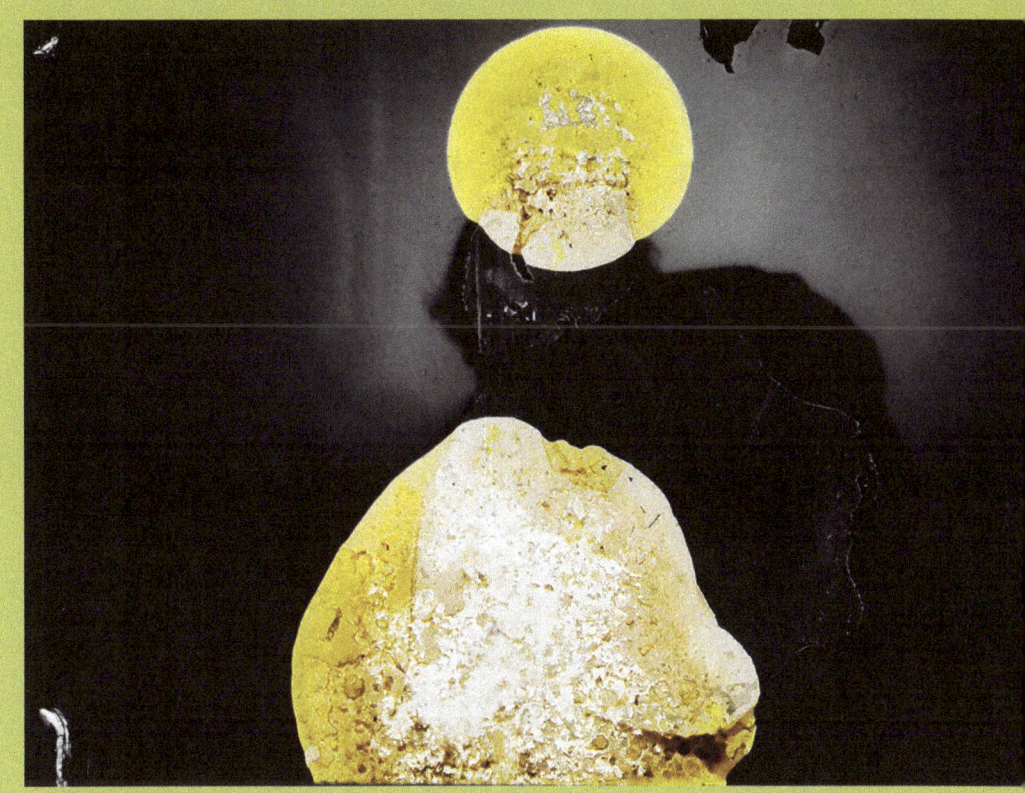

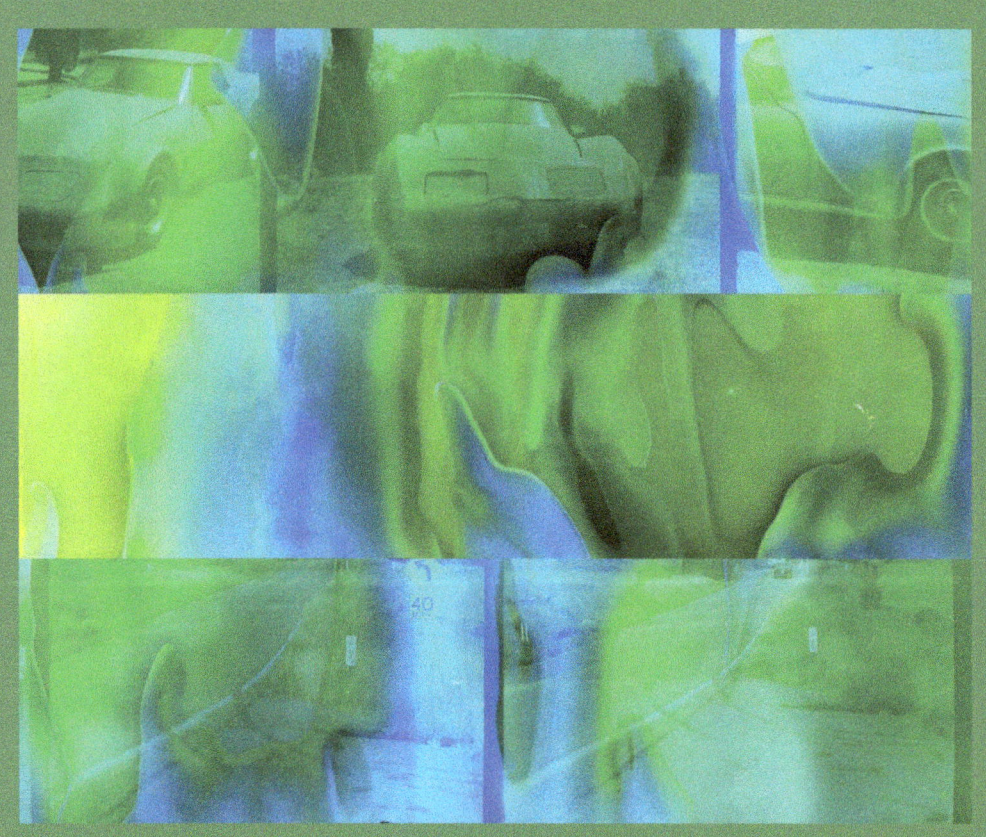

NOLAN BARRY UNTITLED (CAR AND ROAD), 2020 35MM

Nolan Barry

These images are from a roll of Kodak Gold plus 100 that I bought at a swap meet in San Diego. The film had already been shot when I found it, immediately creating a relationship of mystery and alienation. Working with film that I did not shoot has always caused a feeling of uncertainty in ownership of the images. I am simultaneously a thief and a savior.

I brought the film with me back to Chicago where it sat for months before being held again. Eventually, I began wanting to experiment with film emulsion as a means of creating a more complex image. A roll of film that I did not shoot myself gave me the freedom to interfere with the chemistry of the emulsion. I was most excited about doing this tampering before developing the film, anticipating more interesting results.

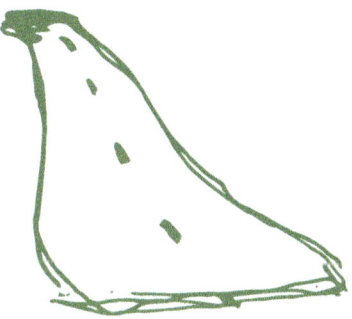

This film was dropped into a pot of boiling water with ¼ cup of citric acid for exactly 3 minutes and 41 seconds. Citric acid was the obvious and convenient choice, as the pH is very acidic, and I already had some in the house. As the acid disrupted the colors of the film and the heat caused the plastic to shrivel, a deep and vivid display of color was born.

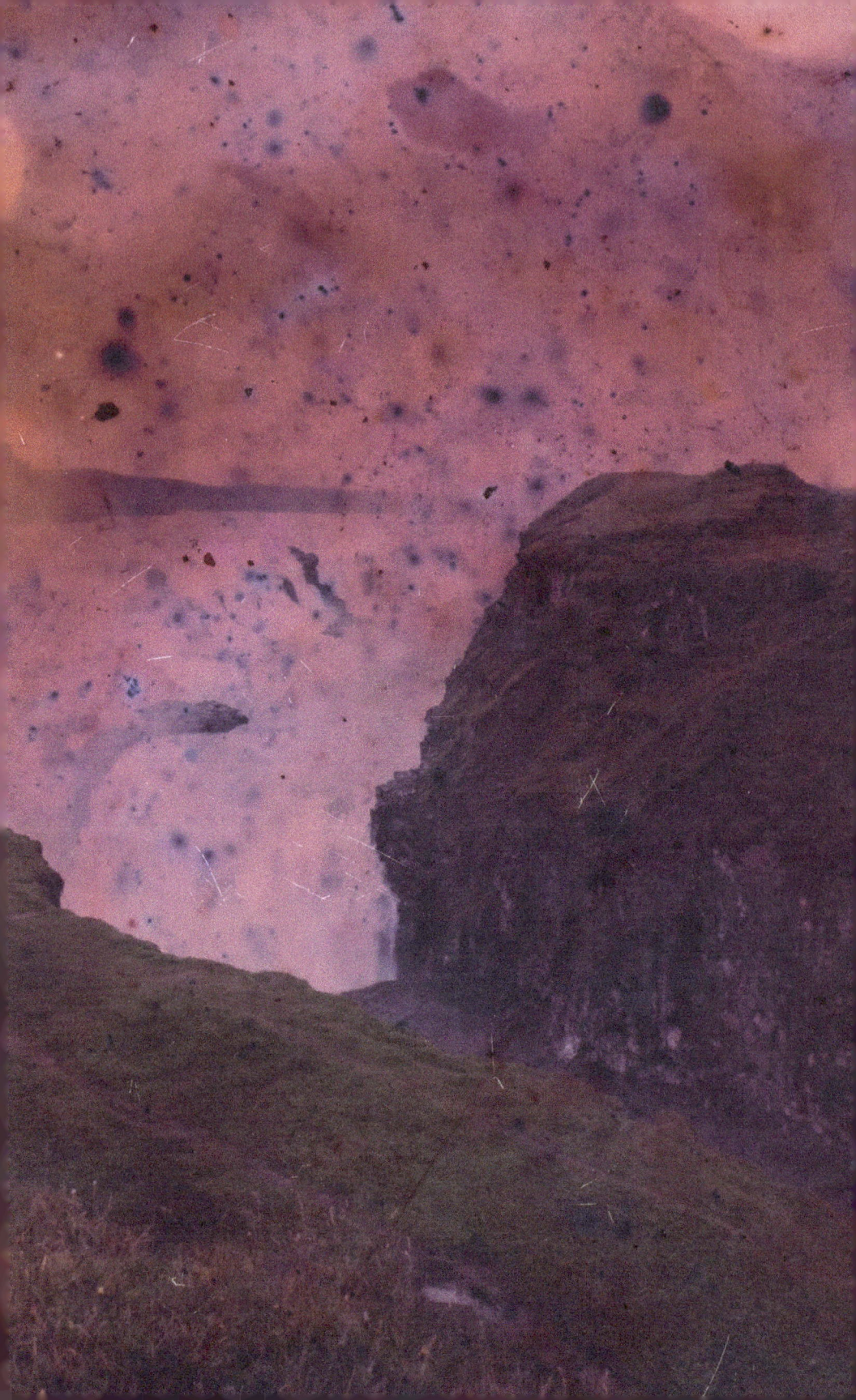

PABLO MARTINEZ-ZARATE

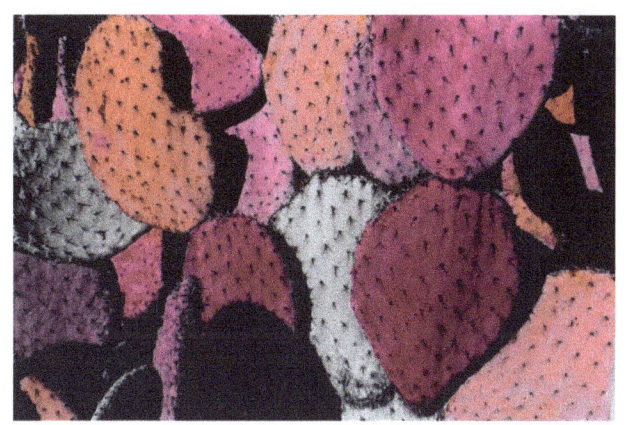

COCHINEAL IN ANALOG FILM

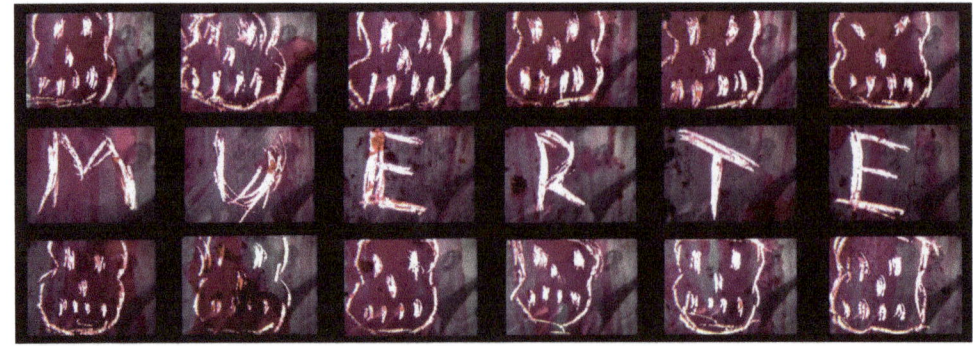

COCHINEAL IN ANALOG FILM AND PHOTOGRAPHY PABLO MARTÍNEZ-ZÁRATE

Dactilopyus coccus, or cochineal, is an insect that grows on the pads of prickly pear cacti, from which a natural carmine dye is extracted. These parasites, whitish when alive, grey when dried, dark red when crushed into powder, were a costly treasure before artificial tinctures were invented. Cochineal is still widely used in food, industrial products and fine textiles created by mexican artisans and designers.

I came to cochineal when trying to represent violence in Mexico through an analogue film and photo project called *These Images Are Truth: Microarchive of Ignominy* (pablomz.info/eisv). The project aimed to translate into images (shot in super 8, 16, 35 and 120 millimeters) the constant denial of facts performed by the official discourse during Enrique Peña Nieto's government (2012-2018). The resulting work has the shape of a small office briefcase-style archive that travels with negatives, positives, dark-room and digital reproductions of the images, as well as a copy of the printed catalogue. The process for this work involved downloading ignominious addresses by the President and members of his circle (such as the press conference regarding the "historical truth" about what happened with the 43 dissapeared students from Ayotzinapa in 2014). For the smallest format (super 8), I worked with three different processes in reversal black and white film; bucket-developed regular positive to generate light scratches; solarized and overexposed (in the developing process as to represent the elusive nature of the analyzed political discourse); and finally, a negative scratched framed by frame and tinted with cochineal as a materialization of violence. The resemblance with blood blew my mind, but the journey with cochineal was only beginning.

An ongoing experimentation with the process has led to implement an array of tonalities that go from carmine to violet or deep purple when mixed with water, and orange when mixed with citric acid. I have applied the dilutions with art brushes directly on film, silver prints, minilab prints, and archival material mainly from texts. I have also applied it with coating and small baths in which to soak the materials. I have also found that, being organic matter, if left humid it can easily develop mould altering the intensity of colors. I call this open research Codex Cochinilla evoking prehispanic Mexican documents (pablomz.info/codexcochinilla).

After a couple of years of research, I still haven't found any previous records on the use of this ancient and precious material in film and photography (nor in print, and I say this because *These Images Are Truth* has a risograph printed catalogue where cochineal was used in a serigraphy-inspired technique). If anyone reads this and knows about other examples of this use, or wants to know more technical matters, I'll be more than happy to hear from you.

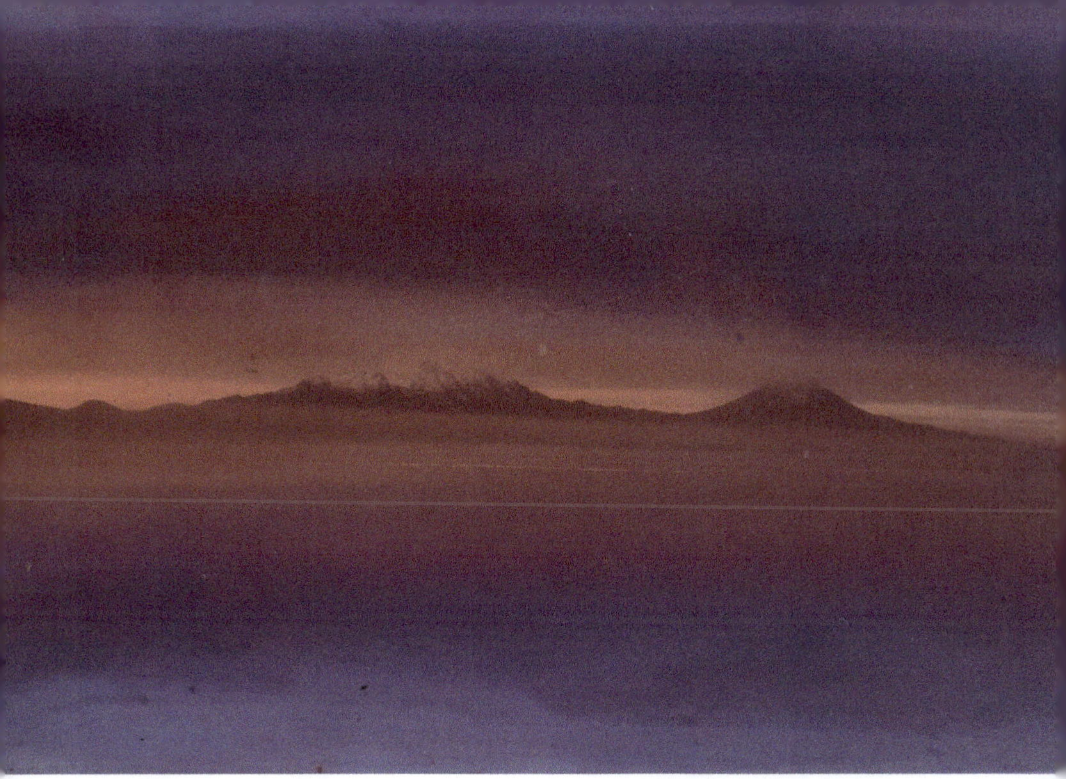

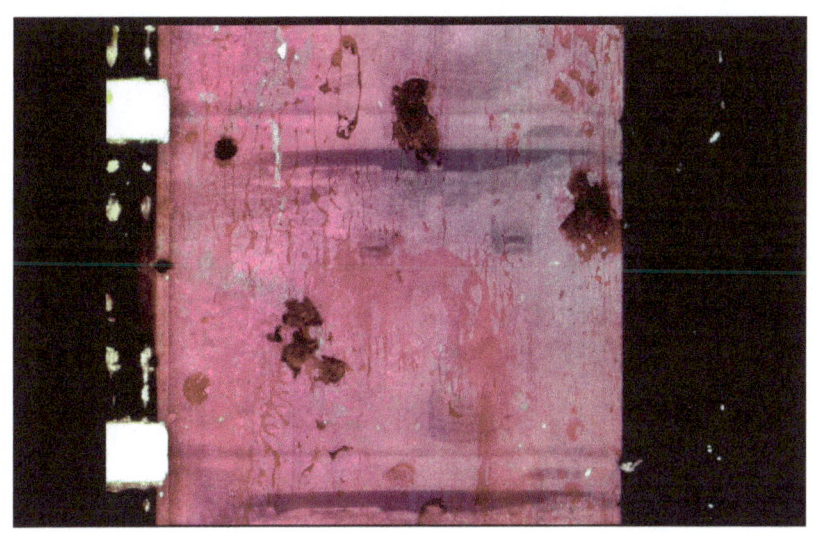

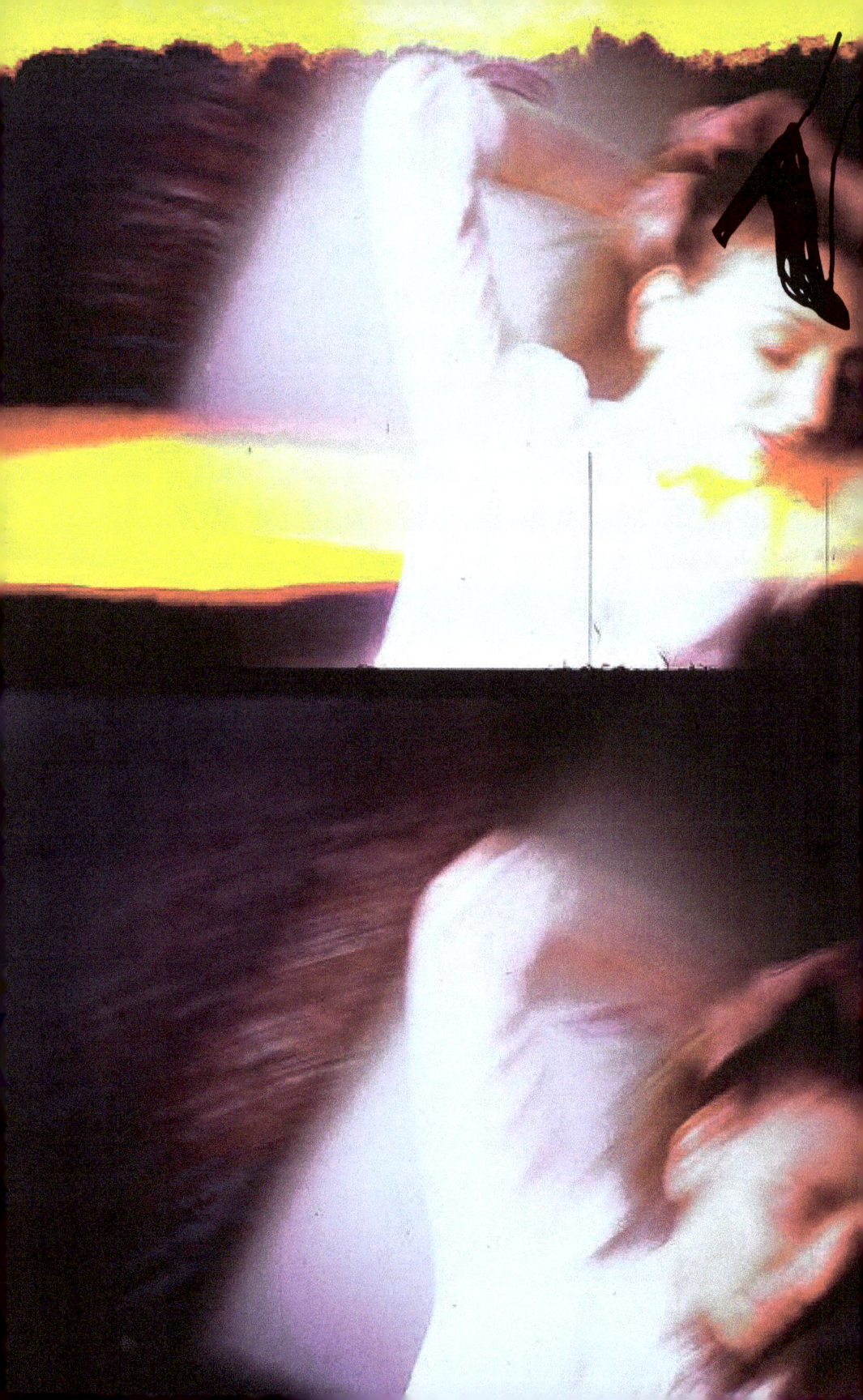

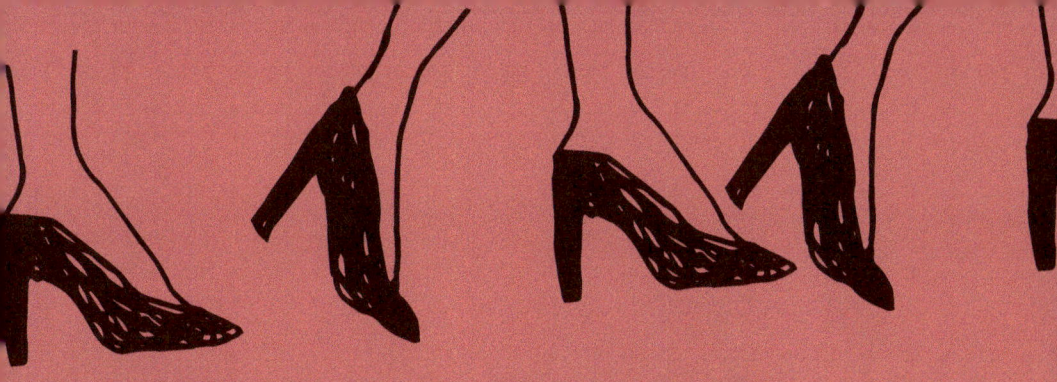

ROBERT C BANKS

These images were all shot with my Bell and Howell Eyemo. The Tiffany series were outtakes from an experimental film I shot in 1999. It was from a B&W Tech Pan film negative that I hand processed and later had printed. The images of Jessica were from Feb 2012, they were shot on long roll slide Fuji color slide film rated at 100 ISO.They were cut into strips and rolled into empty 35mm still cartridges and processed at my local lab around the corner from my studio. The image you selected was used on a Paperback book cover of a collection regional poetry.

I got into photography as a way of exploring creative cinematography and lighting. Doing stuff like this for many years allowed me to test and manipulate exposure, color and motion along with keep a structured theme to my shots. Both sequential and poetic narrative is my goal.

Playing with various chemical processes opened some many doors of making new languages with grays, contrast and textured values of light and color for celluloid filmmaking. Sadly, my allergies kicked in and I can no longer work with photographic chemicals for more than 10 minutes. Man, do I miss that process.

I have many painting, scratching and drawing on 16mm and 35mm film pieces as well.These projects and processes allowed me to discipline my self in the traditional method of film cutting and editing. Which is such a fun process.

I love My Eyemos. They're tough rugged cameras that give the best quality and keep on giving. I own 2. Had them since the mid 90s. I also own a couple Arriflexes, Eclairs, Bolexes, A Bell & Howell 16mm Filmo, loads of Super 8mm and Reg 8mm cameras too.This interest began at the age of 6. Thanks to my late Father. He planted the film seed and it pretty much grew with me.

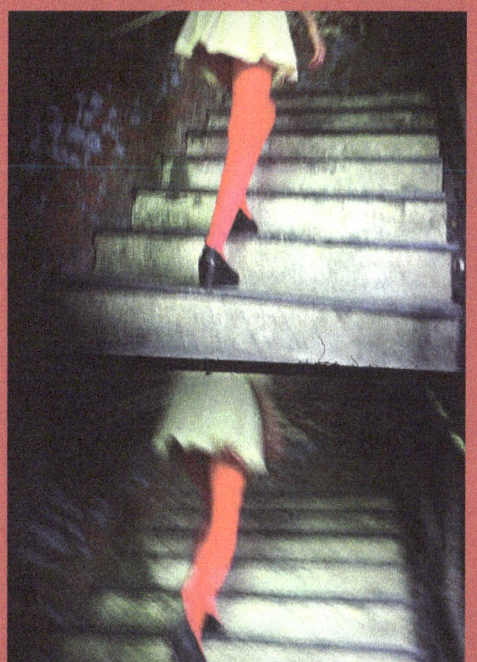

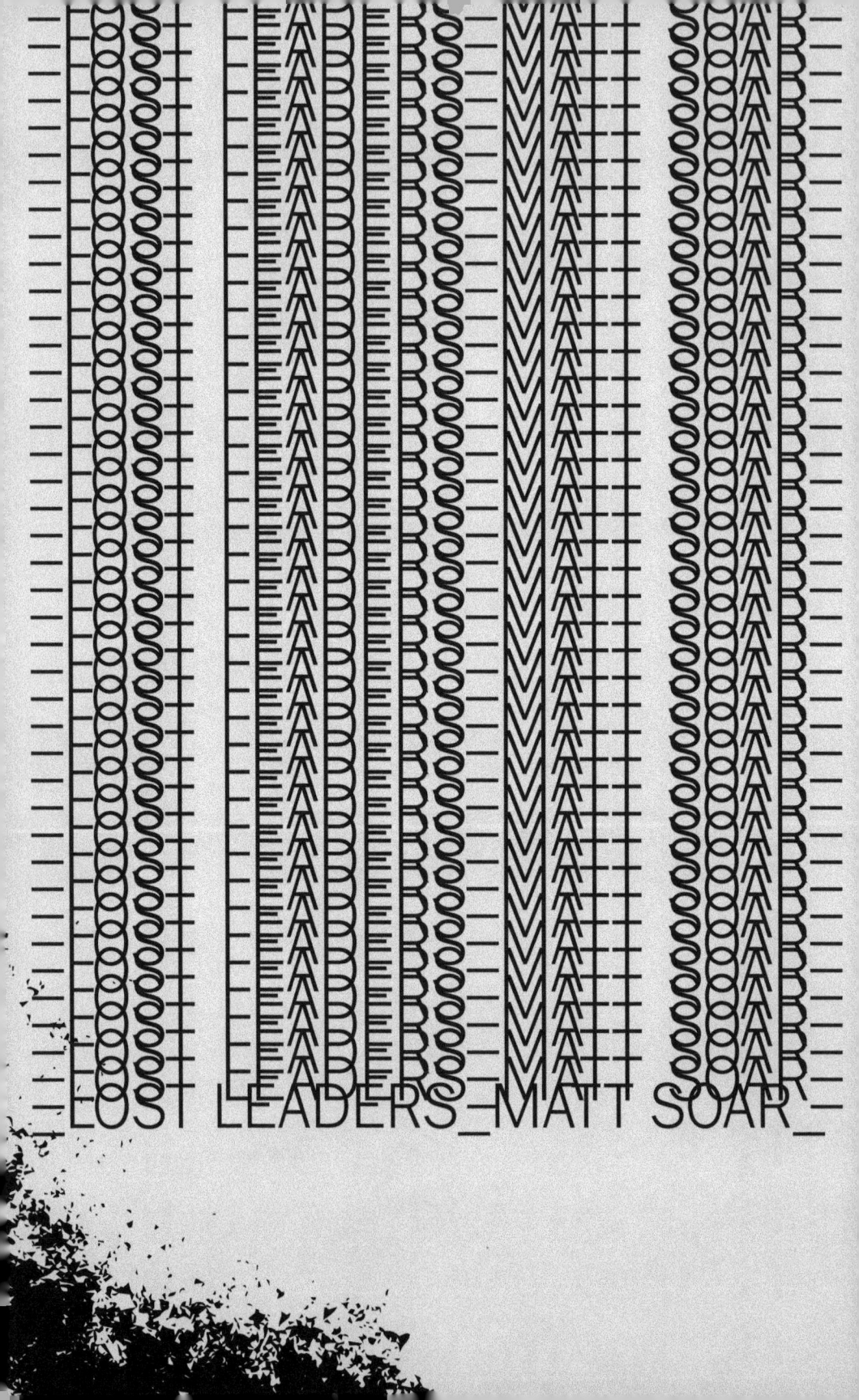

LOST LEADERS_MATT SOAR_

Lost Leaders explores the meanings of commercial film leaders: the generally hidden footage at the beginnings and ends of film reels, littered with all kinds of esoteric markings: countdowns, logos, lab notes, handwriting and type, color tests, projection cues...

...often taking up just a few frames each. Through the project, I propose that leaders are lost in at least three ways: their routine invisibility from the cinema audience; their general absence from accepted preservation and archiving protocols; and, their impending technical obsolescence.

Working with sound artist Jackie Gallant and a variety of tools – a lightbox and a macro lens, a DSLR video camera attached to a high-powered microscope, interactive narrative software, stained glass, direct animation, handpainting, handwriting, handweaving – Lost Leaders is an extended poetic engagement with the metadata of film; the graphical detritus of processing, printing, distribution, and projection.

Origins and Outcomes
In 2011 I was lucky enough to attend the Film Farm, a one-week residential filmmaking workshop run by the inimitable Phil Hoffman. Held at a farm in rural Ontario, the annual workshop emphasizes process and experimentation, using Bolex cameras, high-contrast b/w film stock, hand processing, and Steenbeck editing. One of my own experiments involved a spontaneous decision, as I sat in the barn one day, to start hand-weaving strips of found footage into other pieces of found footage to create unexpected juxtapositions. Some of this material was leader – the sections of film at the beginning and end of a reel, conventionally invisible to cinema audiences, and full of curious markings relating to the film stock and processing, projection requirements, handwritten notes, countdowns, and so on. The outcome was a short I ultimately titled Lost Leaders #1, with a soundtrack added later by artist and collaborator Jackie Gallant.

Returning to Montreal, I soon switched to 35mm found footage, chiefly because it's easier to work with, and easier to find in abundance. One can buy crate-loads of 35mm movie trailers on eBay relatively cheaply. I began creating lightbox compositions – still images comprised of two or three layers of film frames. I also worked with a powerful microscope intended for biological specimens, attached to a DSLR camera. In this way I was able to create short journeys traversing the films' surfaces, and cameraless stopmotion animations reworking some of the textual content of the trailers.

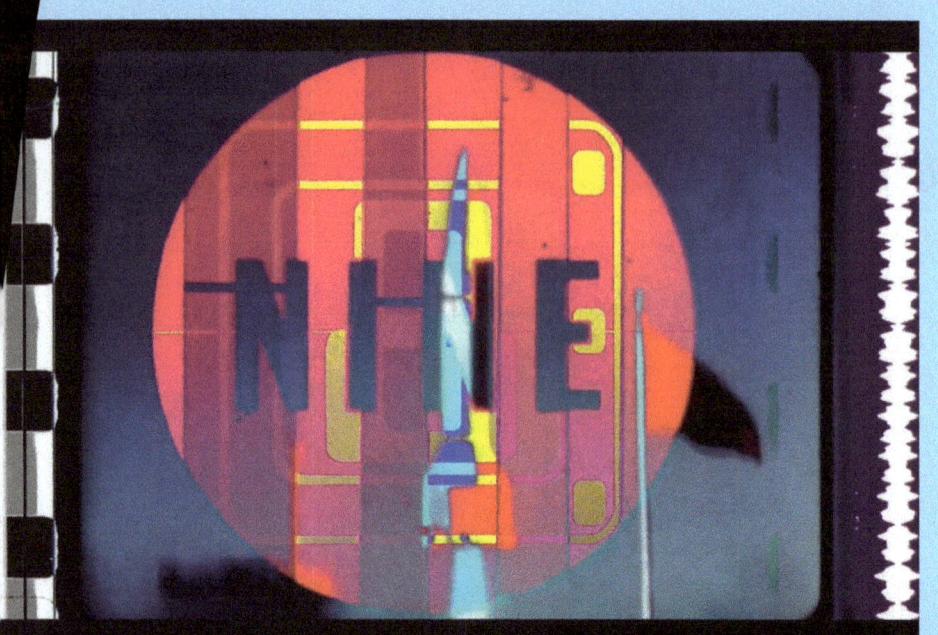

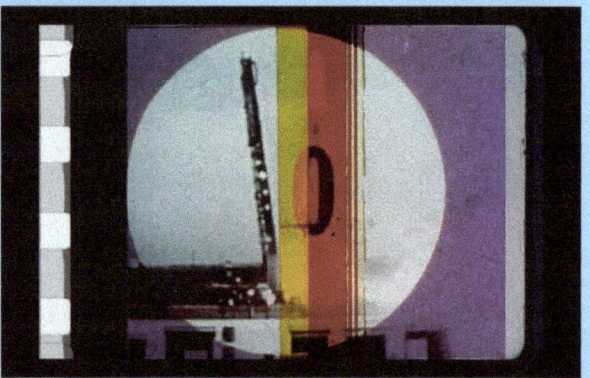

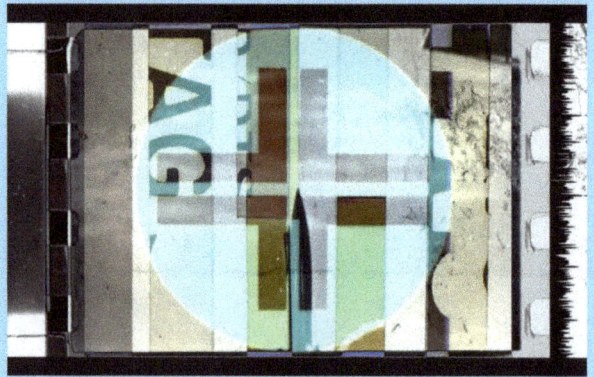

My collaboration with sound artist Jackie Gallant has added a much-needed dimension to the project. Outcomes include an interactive, nonlinear film assembled with the Korsakow System software, in which the user literally plays the film by combining ambient sound, mouseover sound triggered by user interactions, and sound accompanying the videos selected by the user. Academy / Society / Universal: 3 Handwritten Leader Standards (2016) is a three-part, handwritten film, a piece of cameraless animation in which the first three leader standards are drawn by hand, each one followed by the complete text of the associated standard written out on the leader in longhand. This film was first shown at Orphans X (2016, Culpeper VA).

LOVE LEADERS (2018) is best described as a brief, affectionate exploration of the aesthetics of countdown leaders, focusing on films (and one famous TV show) with love in their titles, eg Love and Maturity (1969), Love & Human Remains (1994), I Love Lucy (1954). LOVE LEADERS was created specifically to reflect the theme of the 11th Orphan Film Symposium, held at the Museum of the Moving Image in 2018. Other screenings include ATA/OtherCinema (San Francisco, May 2018), and Engauge Experimental Film Festival (Seattle, Nov 2018). The soundtrack is Perpetuum Mobile by the Penguin Café Orchestra; the peculiar time signature works especially well with countdowns in which the numbers appear at various speeds, eg every 2/3 second (16 frames or 1ft) or every 1 second (24 frames).

ASANASA (2019) combines eccentric countdowns discovered during my archival research, rocket launch footage sourced from Craig Baldwin's 16mm counter-archive, and handwoven leader (see image). This film premiered at ATA/OtherCinema in December 2019, and was most recently shown online in Nicole Baker's Media Monsters Episode 5: Otherworldly Visions (April 2020).

In Summary

In formal terms, Lost Leaders is about exploring (and shamelessly aestheticizing) the paratextual elements of film: the liminal elements of the medium which are not the film per se (ie the thing that directors direct, editors edit, audiences watch, critics critique, and Netflixers download). Conventionally, a movie paratext includes its trailer, promo poster, the DVD cover, and so on. Here, I've interested in what we might call producerly paratexts: the far less obvious facets of a film that are intrinsic to its functioning, but are pointedly not for public consumption. Indeed, leaders are physical traces of a private conversation between lab technicians, distributors and projectionists, and in that sense Lost Leaders can be understood as a tribute to their hidden, under-appreciated labour. Finally, in parallel with these creative forays, I have also written two scholarly essays about leaders. The Beginnings and the Ends of Film in the journal The Moving Image (Fall 2016) describes in great detail the four US/Canadian leader standards developed since 1930. Standardized Film Leaders, a chapter in The Routledge Companion to Media Technology and Obsolescence (2019), explores the multiple appearances of leaders in pop culture, such as in movies, music videos, and graphic design.

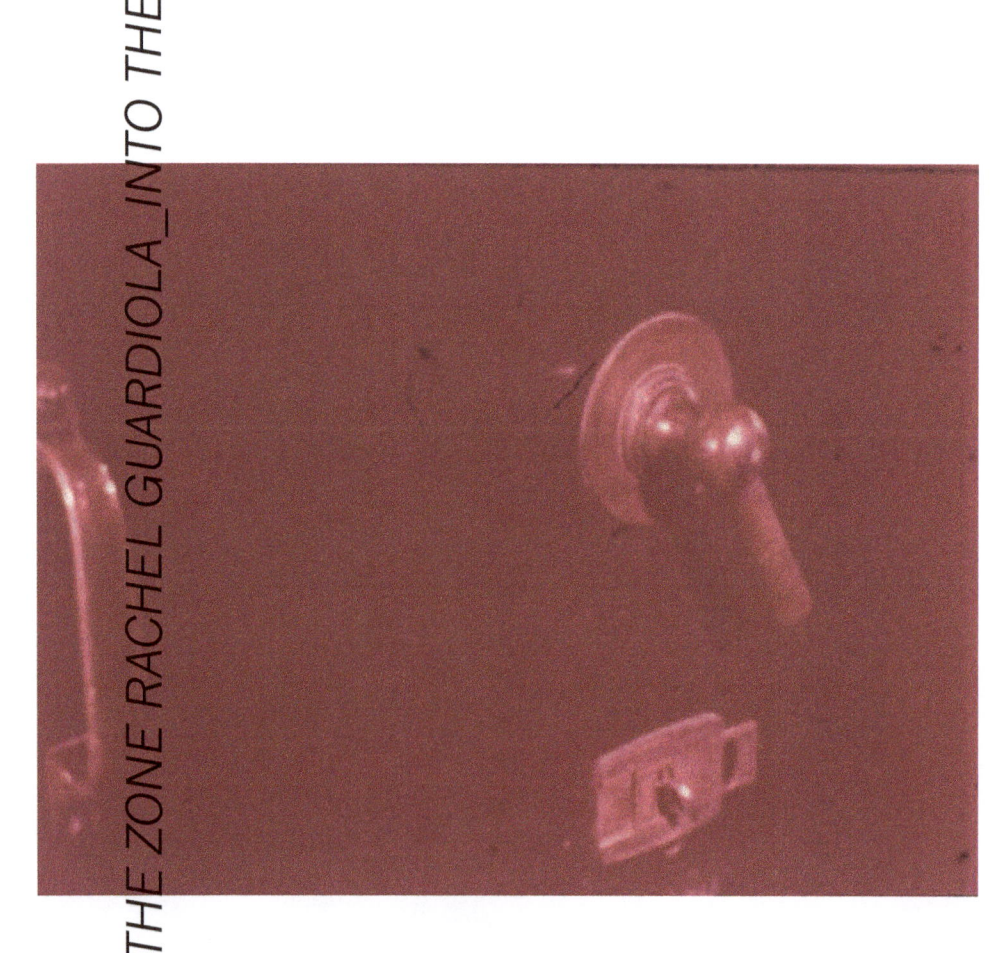

TELL US ABOUT THE INTERSECTION OF NATURALISM AND FILM.

How did you first start exploring human relationships with nature on film?

I have kind of always had an immense double interest in arts and sciences, two things that need complete dedication and are often academically disparate-sometimes even not allowed! I studied visual art but I have worked as a naturalist, taxidermist, and in international agriculture where I spent a lot of time in the desert. It felt like living in two different worlds. I found that walking and navigation were ways that I was able to continue to make work without a studio space and at times outside of an art environment. Functionally, the camera was something I could bring with me, but it also ended up making sense for my work. While walking, I was really interested in the camera's ability to record the first person act of looking, point of view, and rhythm - its ability to mimic the body. I connected this mechanism to the reference point of an onlooker, alien, or other entity navigating uncanny earth like terrains. I do not have a formal background in filmmaking, so I did not realize it was a way of working until later on when I had some really good teachers in graduate school. They also told me that everything I was doing in photo I could also do with film, originally I studied painting. I was also interested in aspects of natural history as a subject, the way archives and categories are constructed – and in the scientific realm, technological inventions used to realize the invisible. In this film, I am hinting at the possibility of what the topography may be after the Holocene Epoch or when humans are the fossils of inspection.

Into The Zone uses a lot of archival material. Where did you find your source materials?

The film consists of original 16 mm black and white film that was captured at a series of different locations - solitary walks at several different outdoor locations, an aquarium, and constructed spaces –filming a small set in my studio and re-filming photographs I captured of these locations. With some of the images, I have used contact printing, bucket, and reversal processing in a black and white photo darkroom. These films are montaged together with some found natural history documentary footage that I had collected. I really wanted to include images like the hands of the lab workers but not their identities – they all look the same - combined with the remix of the generic narrator voice, alludes to the possibility that the content has been found or constructed or replayed by some other entity entirely. The film has been edited to start and end with a curio cabinet as the entry and exit point of travel– similar to old films of tales for children. In exhibition it plays as a loop, so it is meant to seem like a continuous cycle.

Tell us about the hand cranked optical sound. What was that process like?

I am forever in love with the idea of geological time, traveling to natural spaces with no human signifiers - spaces that seem to exist in both past and future. I navigate to these spaces and it is like time traveling for me. The camera enables me to really inhabit these alternate spaces I call 'other earths.' I feel most at home here. The works are usually shown as large projections or installations so that the audience can experience that transport similar to a panoramic painting. With the sound, I wanted to give the feeling of time collapsing, disintegrating, replaying–maybe also some of the nostalgia associated with VCR replay–humans watching nature on TV–humans becoming the subject eventually of the documentary for another entity's viewing and enjoyment. The sound is very much so a remix with specific words brought into focus. I had none of my own equipment at the time and a special film fairy allowed me to borrow their optical sound reader. I hooked the reader up to a digital sound recorder do document it. I played the film kind of like it was an instrument, there was a lot of improvisation, hand cranking the film reels to make different sounds, focusing in on different words, and just really playing with it.

Watching Into The Zone amidst a pandemic left me thinking long and hard about what we leave behind as a species. What do you want your audience to walk away feeling or thinking about?

We may be next and that may not be the worst thing for everything else but us. What the first human saw when they walked the earth.

I am forever in lc
geological time,
spaces with no h

Any other film or photo projects coming up?
In the last month, I relocated to Colorado to teach Photography and Digital Arts at UCCS. I am really excited to be in this particular environment for my work. I am just getting set up here and am finally in a situation where I am able to buy a 16 mm cinematic camera instead of borrowing and am on the hunt for one. I am hoping to begin shooting in some locations in this part of the country and really just have a situation where I can really dive into my work. This past spring after the teaching semester had ended back in NY I was hoping to spend the summer in a community darkroom printing a photo montage series. Due to quarantine this was not possible so I have a lot of stuff up in my noggin ready to be made. I'm hoping to set up a darkroom space at my new home and find a community out here. I maintain a herbarium and have been working on an ongoing project called 'Cryptoflora Field Guide' for some time. It is a book of possible plants that may flourish after humans are gone.

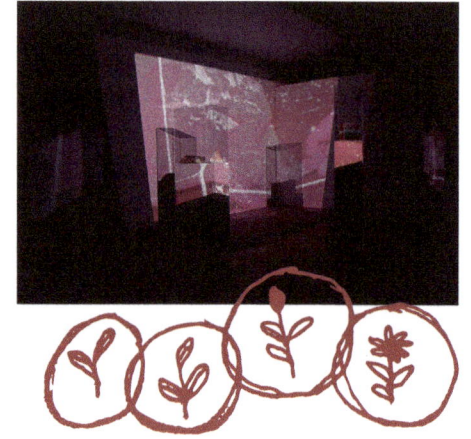

e with the idea of
aveling to natural
man signifiers...

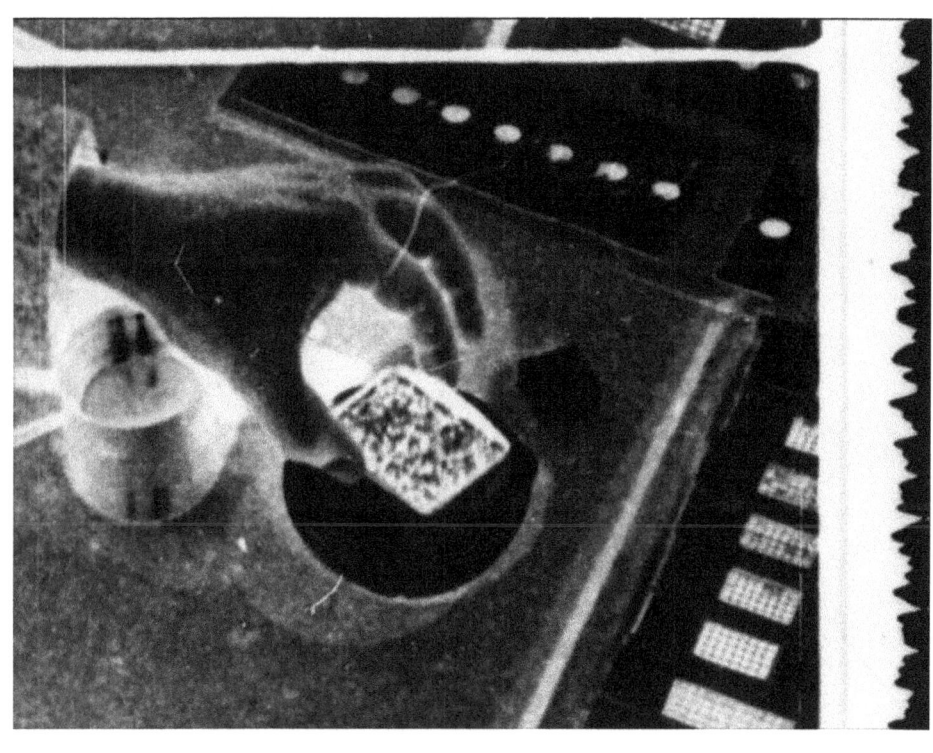

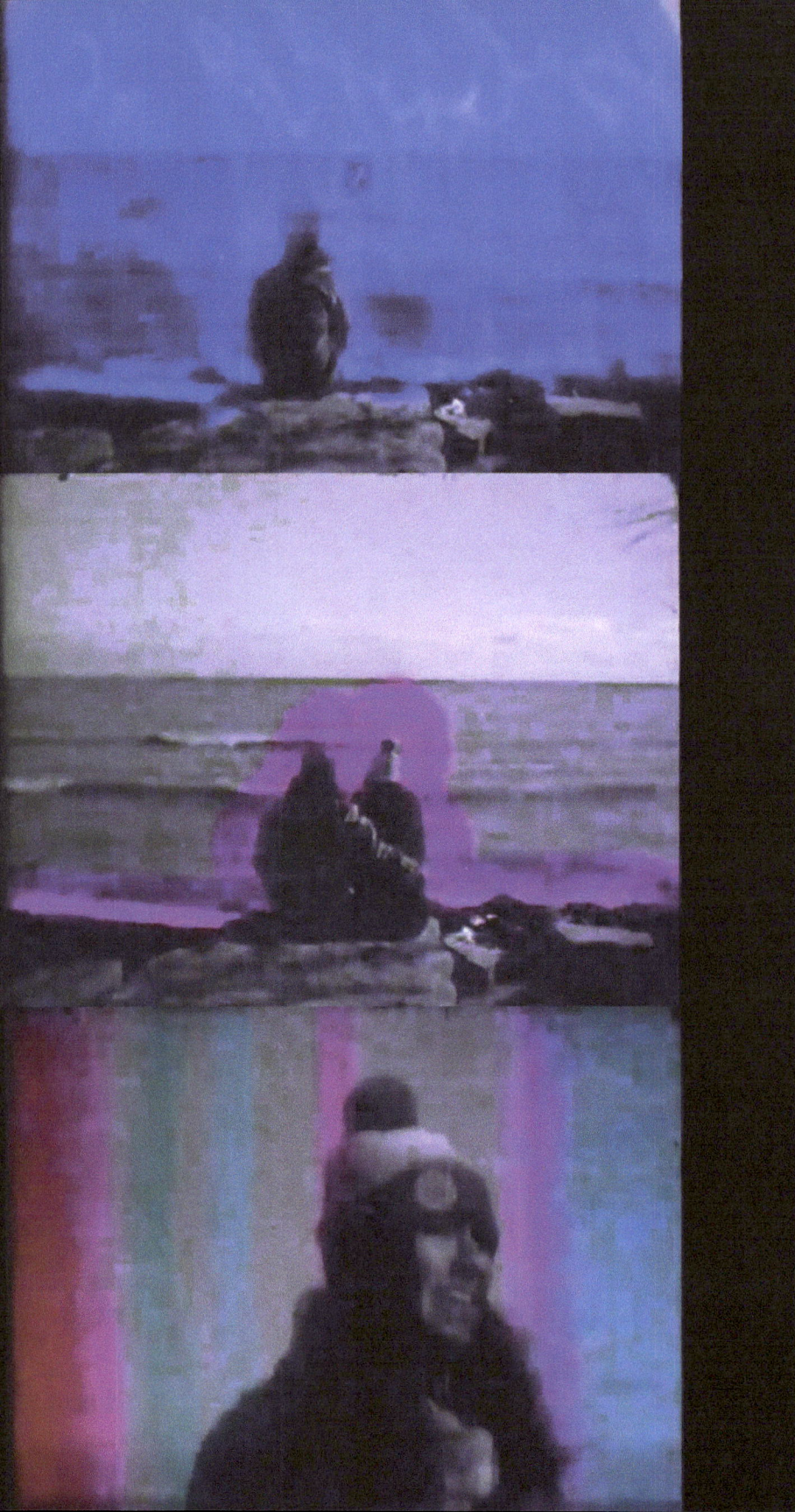

ROBYN EHRLICH

SNAPSHOTS WAS YOUR FIRST PAINTED 16MM FILM. WHAT WAS YOUR FIRST IMPRESSION WORKING WITH 16MM IN THIS WAY?

Before I was ever interested in film and video as an art form, I was extremely invested in the fine arts."I started taking classes at the St. Paul Art Academy when I was seven years old, and eventually taught there between the ages of fourteen and nineteen. My favorite medium is watercolor, but I've done everything from pen and ink, to oil painting, to acrylic. Because of my background in painting, it was exciting for me to incorporate those traditional artistic techniques into my film practice. Color theory was a major focus of mine at the time of making Snapshots, so it was a lot of fun to explore feelings and memories in conjunction with my personal art history. Film is already such a physical medium, and painting directly onto the frames just made it even more tangible for me, which I found important in a piece about grasping onto things that have been lost to time.

Why was it important to revisit years later?

I am not great about going back and rewatching my own work. Most of the time when I watch an older film of mine, I am kind of embarrassed of what I was trying to do, or I wish I could make lots of changes. Revisiting this piece was really special, because I honestly hadn't watched it since I finished it at the end of my very first semester at UW-Milwaukee. Now, almost one year post-graduation, it's taken on a whole new meaning for me. The film was meant to capture the feeling of a fleeting moment, trying to hang on to a memory, but really only remembering the feelings. Looking back now, Snapshots was almost a foreshadowing of what my college experience would be. It's definitely bittersweet.

Who do you look to for artistic inspiration?

The films of Jennifer Proctor were shown to me in an Appropriated Media class a few years ago, and they inspired many of the films I made from that point on. Other filmmakers that inspire me include Karyn Kusama, Anna Biller, Kelly Reichardt, Jennifer Reeder... My favorite contemporary painter is Ines J. (@a.creature on Instagram). The way she depicts bodies and her use of color is phenomenal.

Now that you've graduated, what's next?

It has definitely been a strange time to be a recent graduate (it's also just a weird time to be a human being). For now, I'm still living near Milwaukee, and I'm going to be showing some work this October at the Milwaukee Underground Film Festival and the Milwaukee Twisted Dreams Festival. I recently started a job as the Broadcast Producer at a church on the North Side, so I'm happy I get to be doing video-related work. I'm always making and writing things and looking for new ways to be creative.

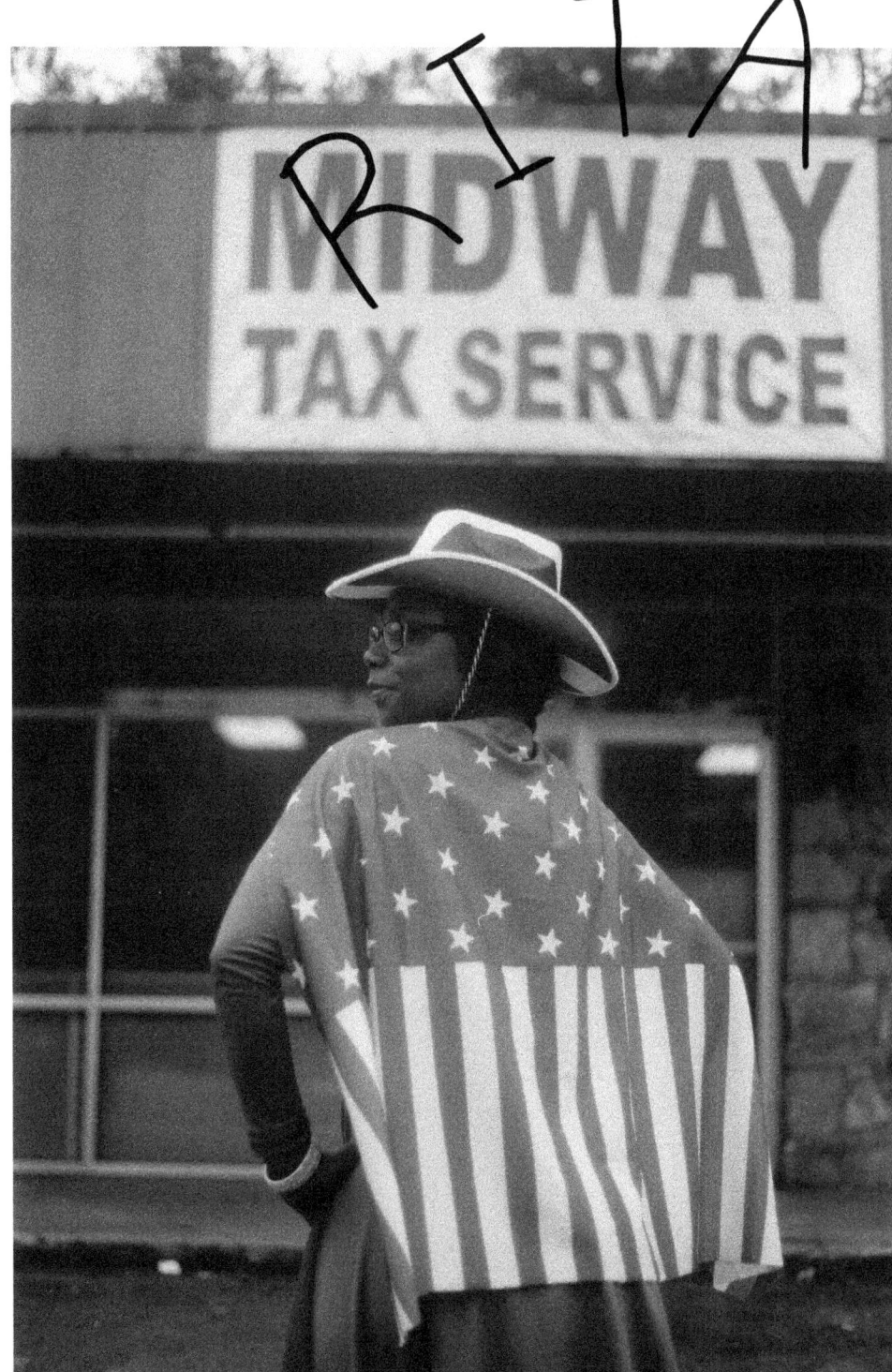

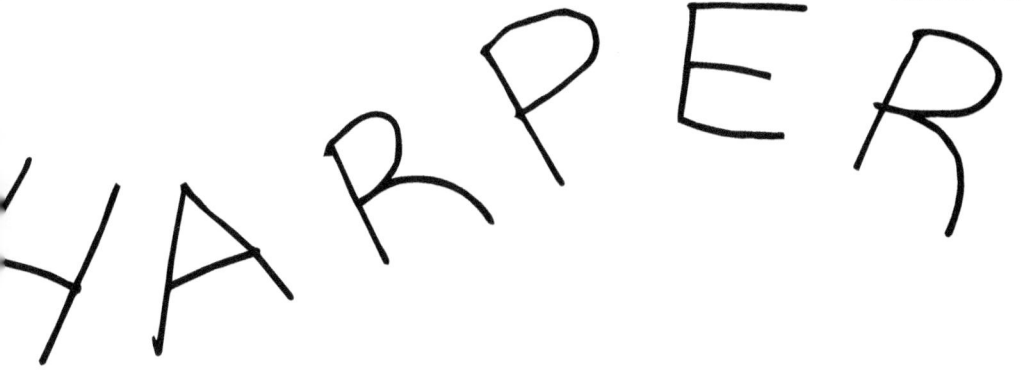

HOW DID YOU GET INTO PHOTOJOURNALISM?

I had been interning at fashion studios, and it just didn't make me feel fulfilled or anything like that. So, I just had to really search and say, "Who am I? What do I really want to express?" That's when I started to go out and document. I fell in love with going out and interacting with people, getting their stories and just being able to celebrate them visually.

Did you start off with film or did you start off with digital?

I started off shooting digitally and then I would see these photographs online. They just had such a different texture, such a different look, and I was really curious as to what that was. Then when I discovered it was film. I started shooting film and then switching over to journalism and documentary at the same time. Once I started shooting film, I was hooked. I was like, "I never want to shoot digital again." It was just magical, honestly, being able to go out, trust yourself, having to use your intuition to understand, "Okay, you know what? I got it," and trusting yourself like that. Then just that element of surprise from the film, getting your film back, and then going out and not knowing what I was going to get when I went out and documenting. It was just such a thrill.

You have a really distinct color palette in your color photos. Can you tell us more about that?

When I started shooting, I was mostly shooting 35mm black and white. I love black and white so much. I love the classic-ness to it, the drama of it.

I realized there's a lot of value in black and white, but then I started to realize the value of color and how it can feel like you're literally right there. Even when we talk about protest photography–if you look at it, it can make it seem relevant, but when you look at it in black and white, it seems like it was decades ago.

I like really low light, low ISO films. I started with Portra 160 and then Ektar 100. Those are probably my two favorite color films. But I recently started medium format. In medium format I like Portra 800 a lot. Black and white, there's a lot of value in it, but I'm realizing there's a lot of value in color too.

Do you identify as a documentary photographer or do you have a specific way you identify your work?

I would say I'm a documentary photographer/ photo journalist. I go out and I document my neighborhood, but I also really love doing photo stories. The documentary film that I'm doing is about a TaeKwonDo master, but it's based off a photo story that I did on a TaeKwonDo master who's losing his facility due to COVID-19. That's why I will call myself a photo journalist as well, because I do like going out and getting those intimate stories in my neighborhood, or just of everyday people and their businesses, or their life journey, or just the circumstances that made them who they are.

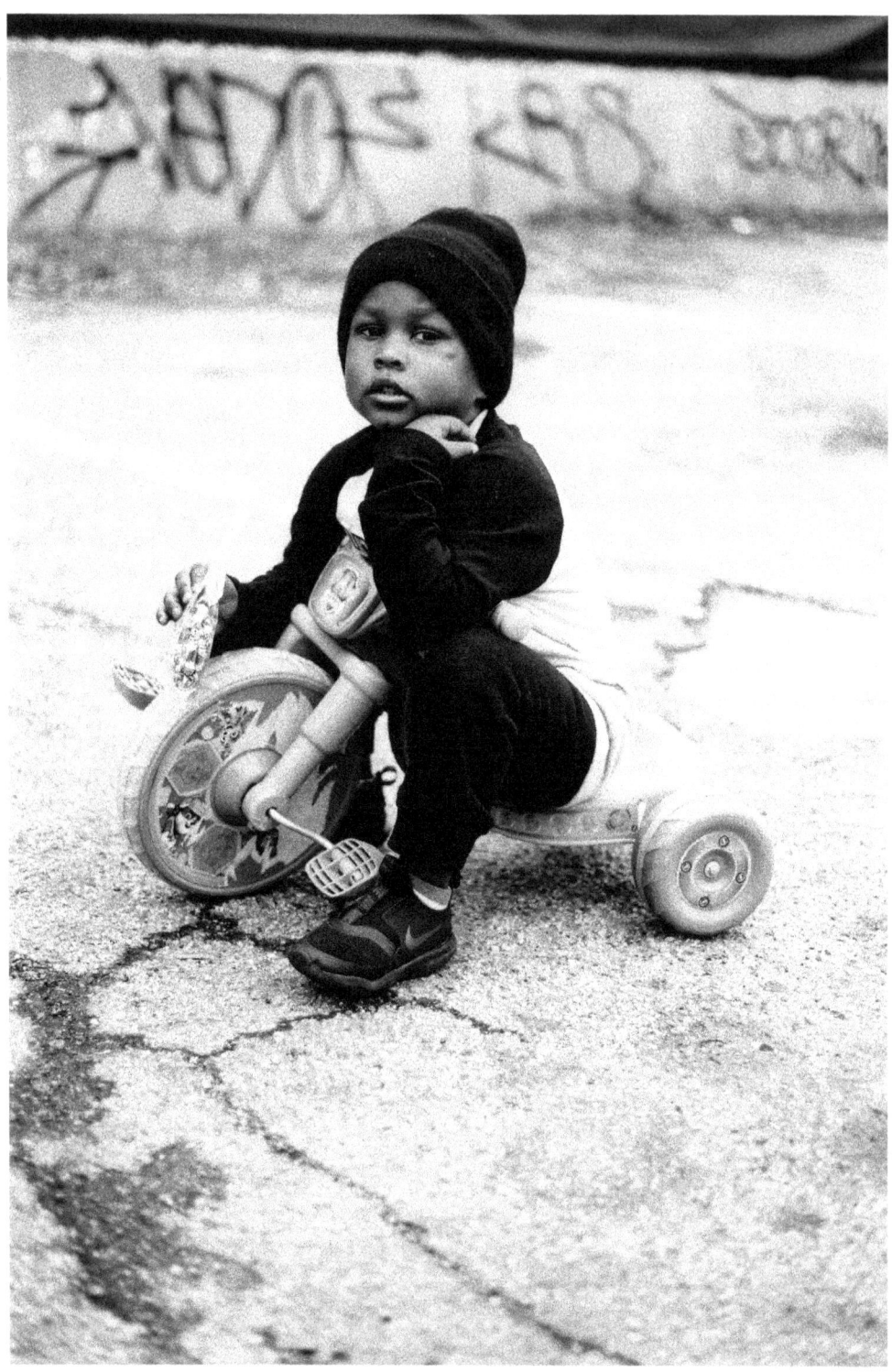

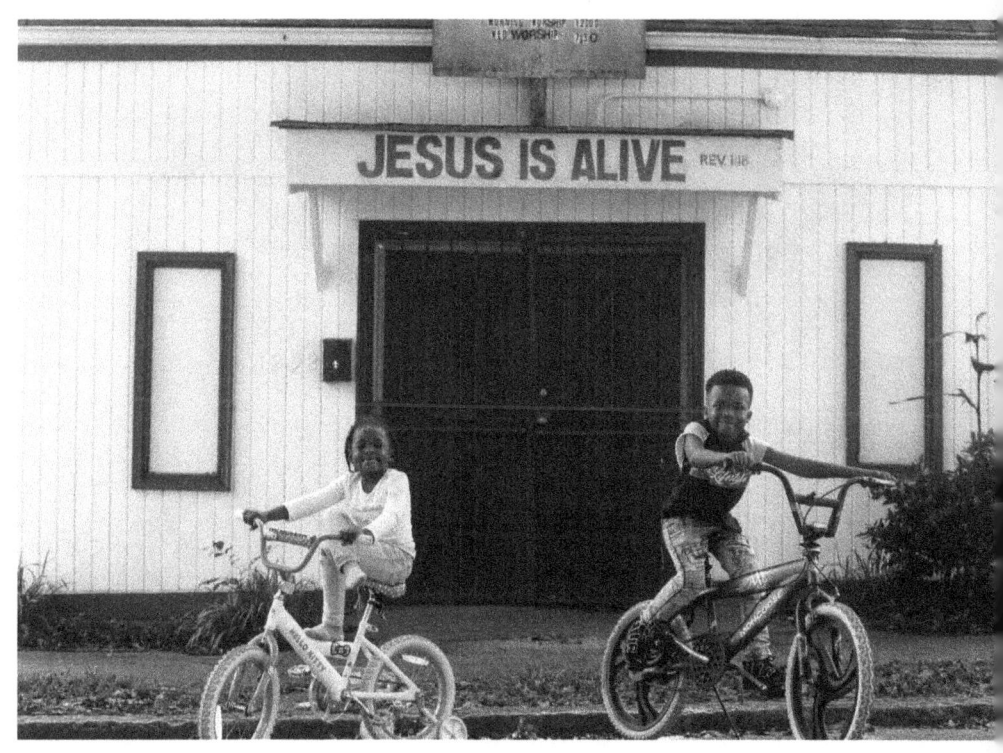

What neighborhoods in Atlanta do you document?

Mostly all of my documentary photos, I would say, are either between East Point, the Cleveland Avenue area, West End, and downtown. It's really places that natives would think to go to. I try to shoot from that point of capturing just what everyday life is like for me.

What is your go-to camera?

My baby is my Olympus OM-1. That was the camera that my friend recommended for me to get to start with, and I got it from Wing's Camera at a really good discount. The OM-1 has really good quality. I feel like it has a unique characteristic to the lens. It's has a 50mm Zuiko lens on it. That's my go-to, because it's super light.

I can take it with me everywhere and it's not a burden, because it's so light. When I'm going out in the streets and documenting, then I want to grab my OM-1. Then if I see someone I can quickly pull it out. Sometimes if I'm riding around, I'll bring my RB67 with me and have it in the car in case I see a scene that just it's like, "Okay, it needs to be larger." For the most part, my go to is the OM-1. Then, if I'm doing an actual photo story, like an editorial story, then I'll probably use my RB67.

How are you finding the people that you want to profile? Are you just going up to people and talking to them or is it more premeditated?

It's very interesting. Honestly, all of my best shots have come by total surprise. The photo of the woman who's by the MARTA station–I got off the train and then she just walked past me. She just had this confidence that was just hypnotizing. Then I just stopped her and said, "Hey, can I get your photo?" I just honestly let people be themselves.

She just pretty much posed herself, and just hit this pose that was just so powerful, and then I got it.

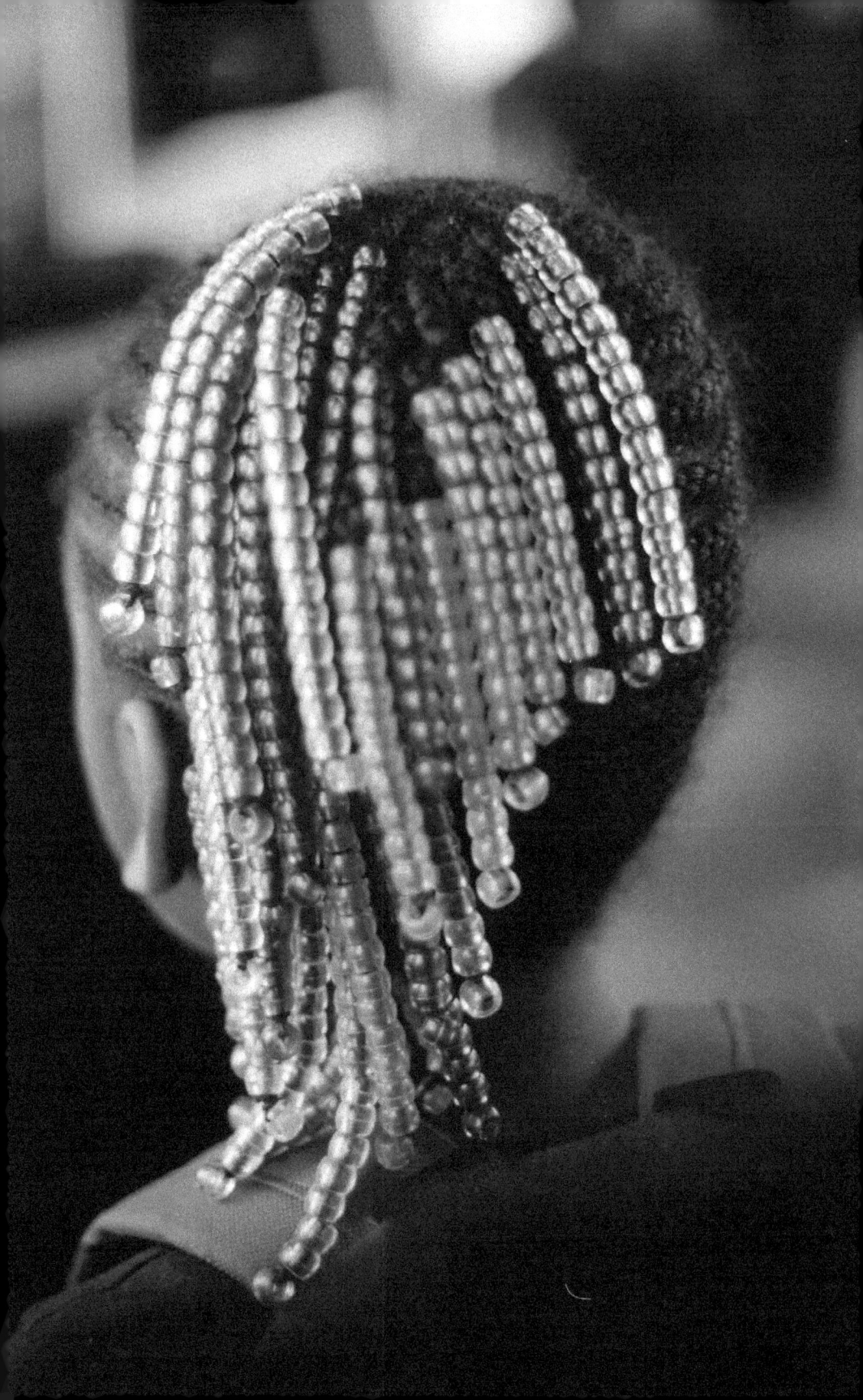

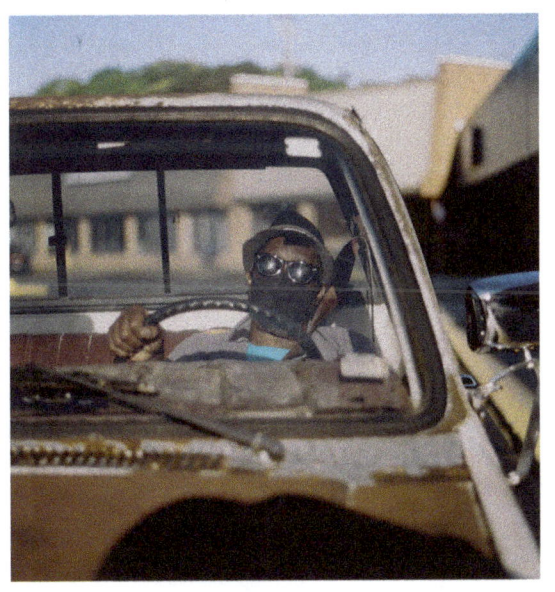
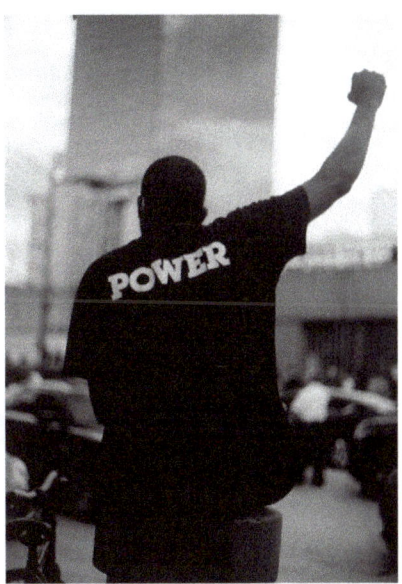

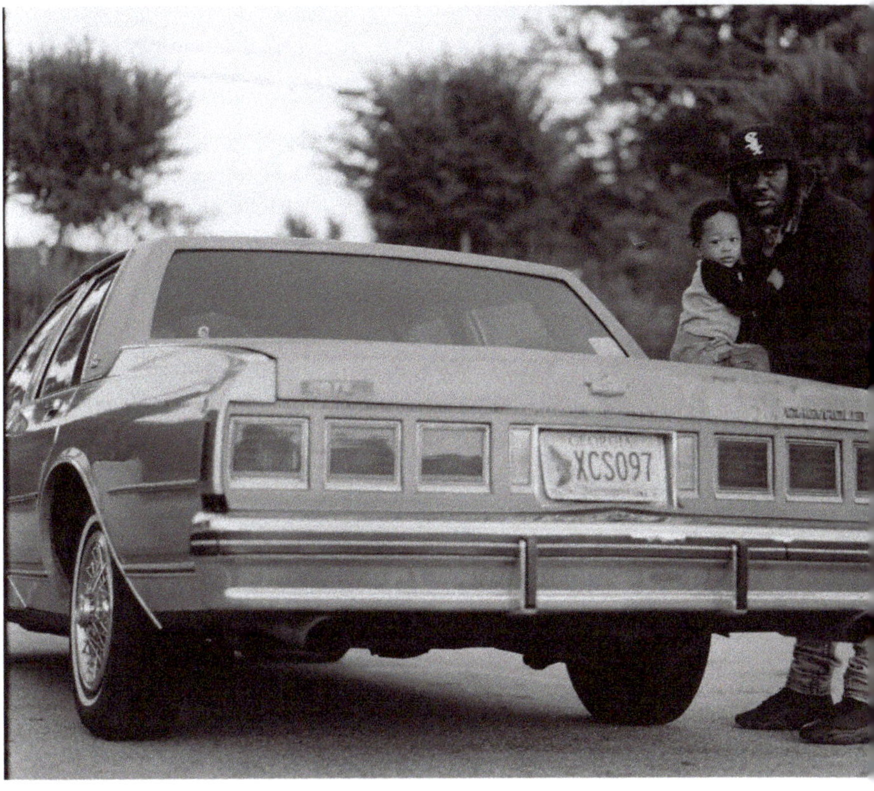

My best photos come from surprise. I never know. I don't have it premeditated. I just see someone that intrigues me, or I see a scene that I think looks dope or beautiful, or I come across someone who I just think has a dope spirit or dope aesthetic. I just usually stop and ask them for their photo.

You just published a coffee table book of your work in February.

Yeah, I called it Still Light. It was a play on words–still light in photography, you're capturing in still light. Then still light just for the people, dedicated to them. No matter what you're going through, no matter where you are in your life, even if you're in that transitional period, you're still light and you're still deserving of recognition and praise.

I feel like sometimes we celebrate celebrities or things that society has told us hold value. Then, where is the everyday person making their way through life left in that narrative?

What does that do to the psyche of the everyday person who haven't reached that level yet? You still hold purpose just simply for existing. I'm a big believer in that. I think that the people I come across, they have something to their spirit that is just so beautiful, and they still deserve to be celebrated. I think that's what that book represented to me.

What have been some of the reactions to sharing your photos with your subjects?

They love it. I think one of the best reactions I got, I took a photo of this couple on the train, which was very dope because this was on Juneteenth. There were a lot of protests and everything like that. During that whole time, I was still trying to figure out, "Where does my visual voice come through in this time as far as protests." They was just the cutest young couple. You could just feel their energy. They were really, really in love. You know the purity of that teenage love. It's so innocent. I sent that photo to them and they absolutely loved it. They want to get a print and everything.

Given the protests and pandemic, has your process changed?

I definitely feel a duty to go out and capture my neighborhood. I've always been capturing it, but I had to find my place in the ecosystem visually. For me, I realized I love going to the protests but something about capturing the protest, there's a lot of trauma there. So, I had to find my place. I had to say, "Well, you know what? You're still documenting and showing everyday black life in a positive way, there's still value in resistance and revolution in that way."

It's hard I love going out to the protest, but capturing the protest, something about it emotionally just didn't resonate with me that well. But still being able to go out in my neighborhood, and showing us when we're not in a state of crisis, and we're not in a state of trauma, was very relieving for me. I love to be able to add to the visual narrative that way of what's going on during that time. I had to find out my place and what I could offer.

Anything else to add?

I love documenting Atlanta, but I do want to branch out too. I want to go to different places and document black life in other states and other places. That's more of my future goals–to expand beyond Atlanta, and see what's going on in New Orleans, Houston, DC, etc.

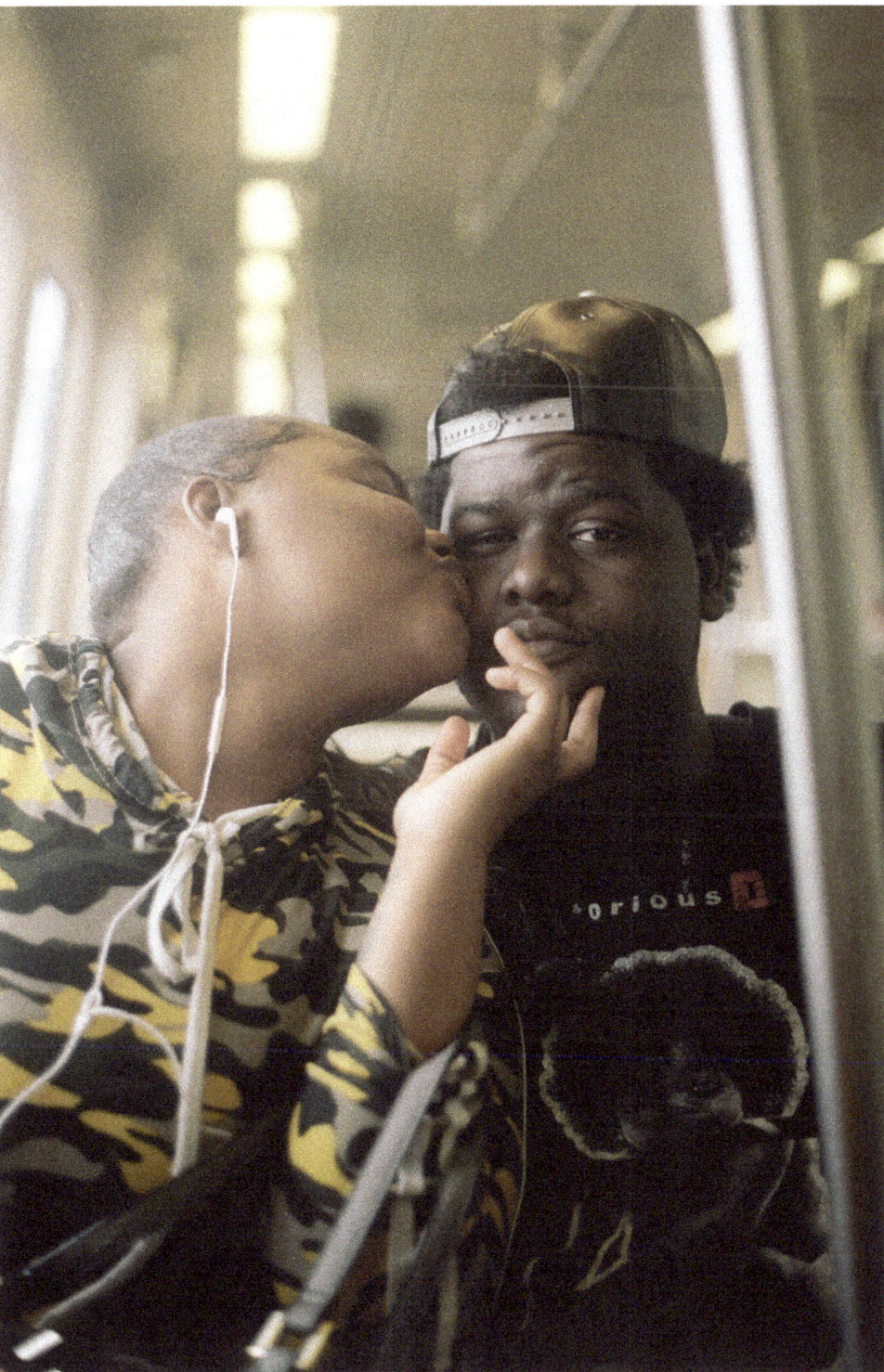

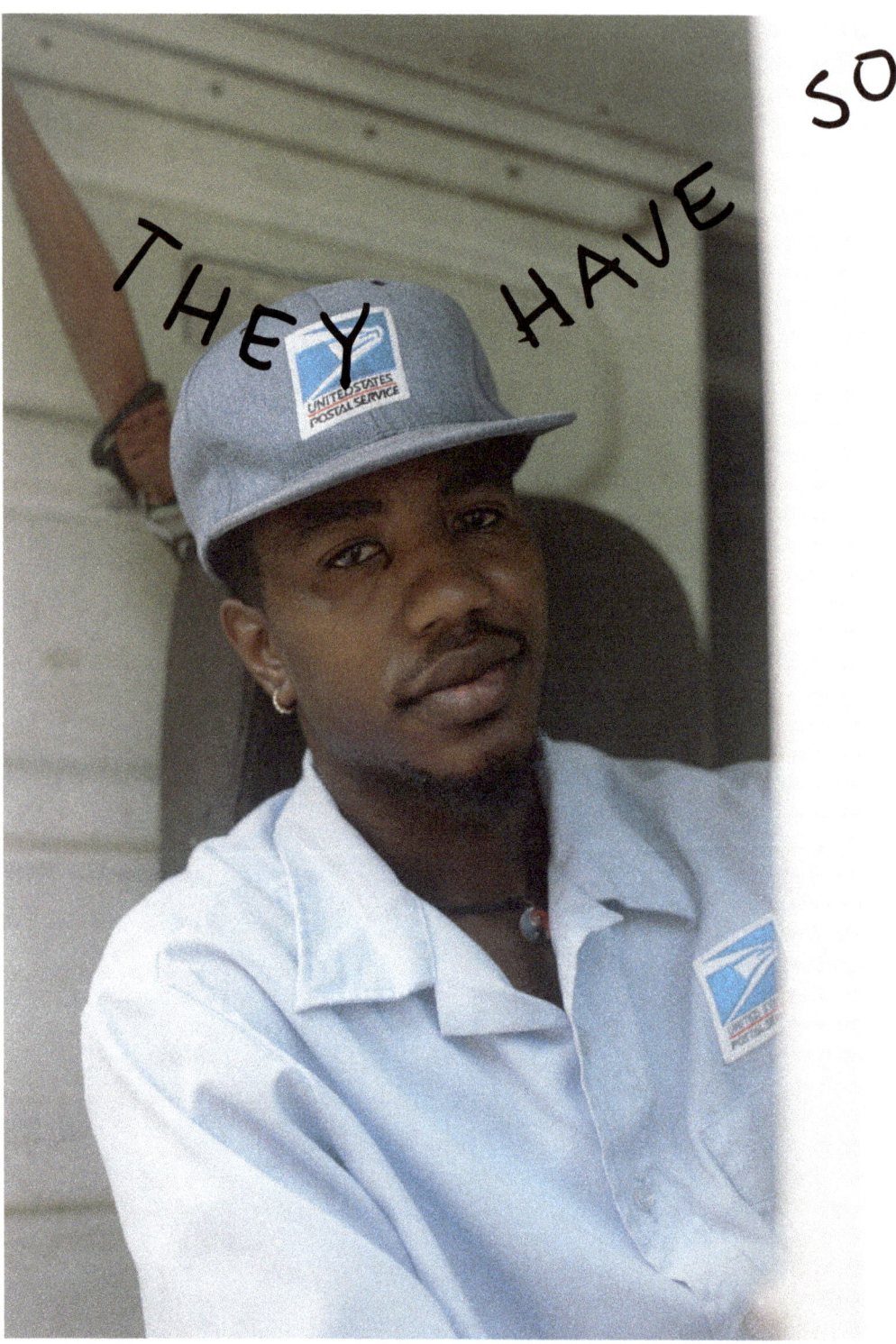

THEY HAVE SO

THING TO THEIR SPIRIT

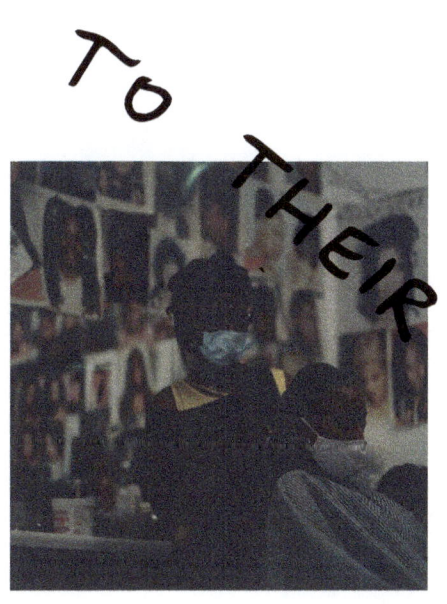

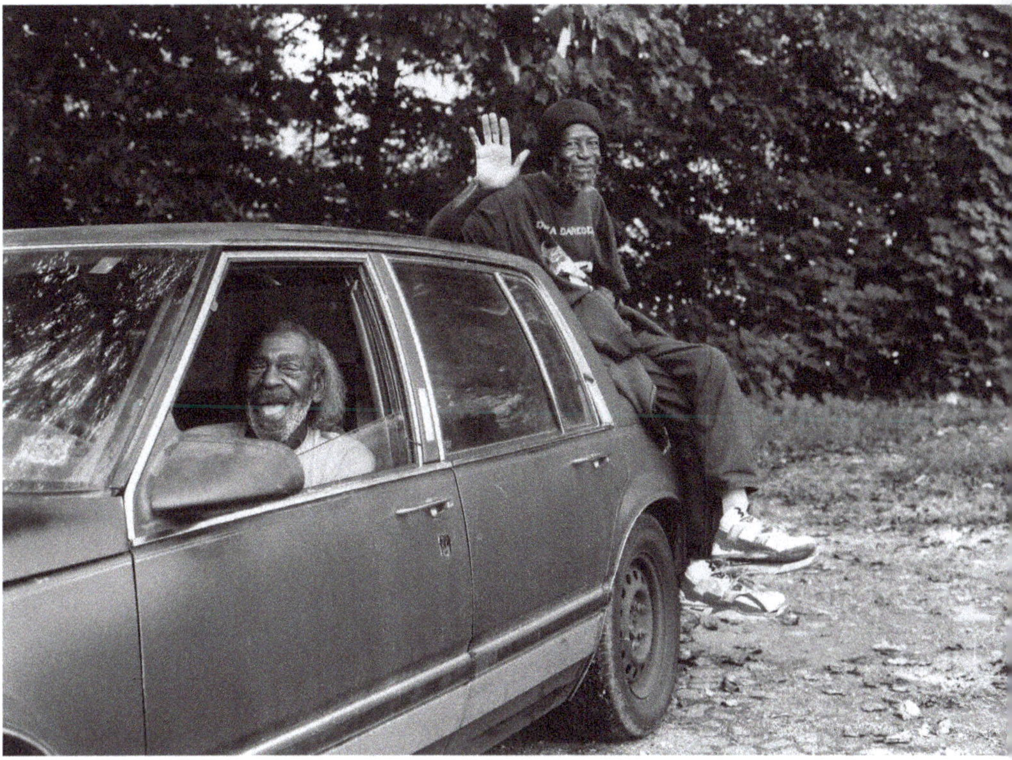

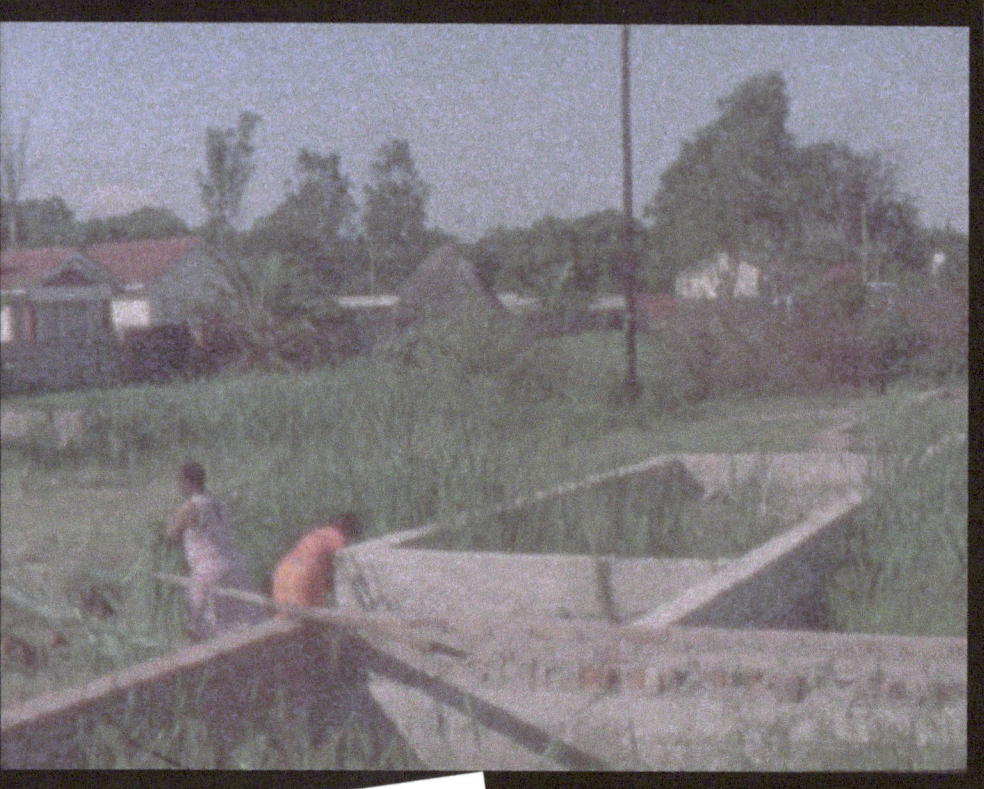

ROGER HORN

SCENES FROM A

TRANSIENT HOME

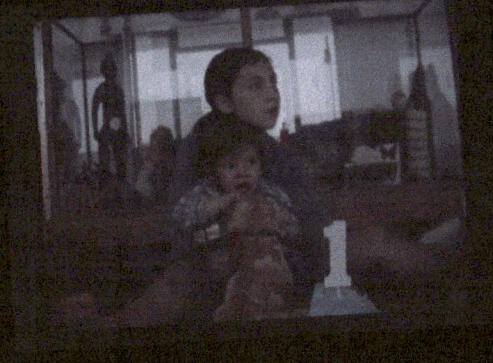
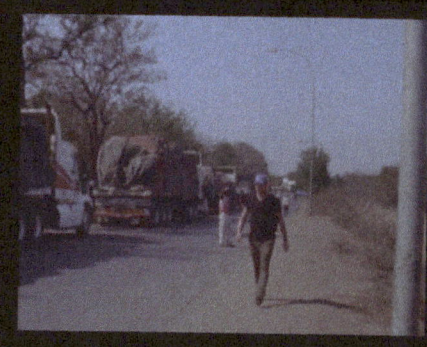

FILMED ON SUPER 8MM, SCENES FROM A TRANSIENT HOME PRESENTS A FRACTURED PORTRAIT OF LIFE FOR ZIMBABWEAN MIGRANTS WHEN THEY TRAVEL BACK HOME TO VISIT.

What's your background as a filmmaker-anthropologist?

A couple of lives ago, I was an actor. I grew up in Nashville. All of a sudden, at 19 I wanted to be an actor, so I moved to Los Angeles. And actually, it was going quite well. But then, I started working production. I worked on everything you can imagine–commercials, indie films, reality TV. But reality TV really leads me to where I am now. The ethical issues with it were ridiculous. And as I slowly started getting a little bit older and wiser, I couldn't believe what these shows were doing.

I ended up moving to Cape Town and seeing everything that was going on there really made me want to change and start making documentaries. So, I made The Sisterhood (2010) and at the same time I released a film on the xenophobic attacks in 2008, in Cape Town. When I made those films, they both did quite well. I went back to L.A. and hoped I could maybe have some kind of a documentary career.

And I did, but it was right back into the same stuff. So, I decided to go back to school. I found a Masters in Visual Media Anthropology in Berlin. And it was just everything I've ever been interested in since I was a kid.

Once I did the Masters, we had a couple of professors that were really interested in the crossroads between visual anthropology and experimental film. And I really took to that. That's when I decided how I really wanted to make films.

When thinking about anthropology or ethnography there's usually a distance between subject and interviewer, but you include your voice narration in the piece as a filmmaker. We see you with a camera and your reflection, and those little moments all draw attention to your perspective throughout the film. Can you talk a little bit about this artistic choice?

It's such a big thing, anthropology with its colonial roots. Everything was very hidden. You never really even see the filmmakers, and everything was expected to be taken as truth. For me, it's really important to point out in the films that it's just a small piece of what I'm observing and seeing, and that's why Scenes from a Transient Home is that way, of course. It's important to me. Especially I'm not from Africa. I'm a white, male, tall, weird, tattooed researcher, and I think it's important to put those things in. I'm not trying to speak for all Africans. I hope everyone always feels when they watch the film that it's what I've gathered.

85

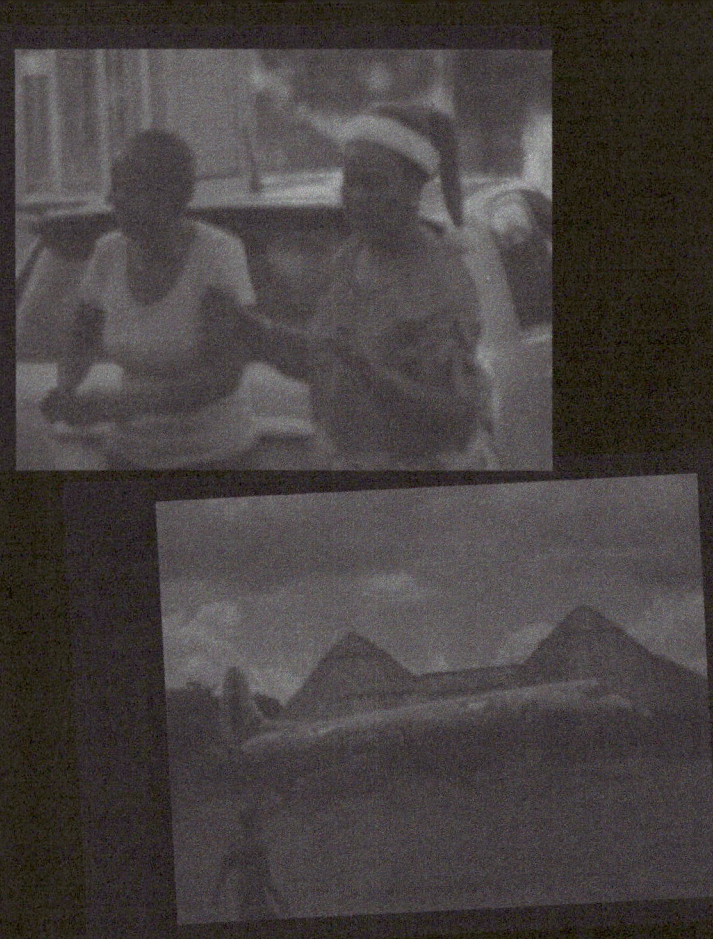

Tell us about your process making *Scenes from a Transient Home*.
 I used found home movies from Cape Town and colonial Rhodesia. The first half is my reflections on the research and how I've been watched, and the second half, the women in the film are asking me questions about the souvenirs I brought back, but all while this colonial footage is playing.

I really have a problem separating life, art, and research. They just always become really wrapped up in each other. I'm fully involved. I can't make a film about anyone and not just almost fully be a part of their lives. I can't do this parachute research. I can't just pick a spot on a map and say, "I'm going got go to Bangladesh," and spend a year and then come home and just share this information with nothing but my American or European friends, and forget about it. I feel too much responsibility.

You used Kodachrome, an expired film stock that can be difficult to process nowadays.
 I sent that to Film Rescue International in Canada and they got the image. I had this thing in my head that I'm going to shoot Victoria Falls and the footage probably won't turn out. Victoria Falls is kind of like this European tourist destination. It shouldn't even really be called Victoria Falls. It's Mosi-oa-Tunya. That's the

Shona name for it–The Smoke That Thunders.

And I'm thinking if it doesn't turn out, I also think that's amazing because the majority of Zimbabweans never get to see Victoria Falls, so it would be kind of amazing if my only memories of the falls were some black static and fuzz.

The film brings up the statue at Victoria Falls of David Livingstone. It's interesting watching this film when all these statues are currently being removed in the United States.

It's crazy, David Livingstone "founded" Victoria falls in 1855. When he got here, there were over 100,000 inhabitants. No one mentions that. It's bizarre because of former prime minister Robert Mugabe's policies. He did everything he could to run every white person out, but he left the statue and he never touched Cecil Rhode's grave. Rhodes is buried in the Matobo Hills, which has significant meaning to Shona people. He never touched his body. He left him there. It's also with the contradictions of Mugabe and his anti-Wes and anti-white rhetoric. The only thing bringing tourist money into Zimbabwe at the moment is Victoria Falls. He leaves this Livingstone statue. It's really bizarre.

I have another film that is coming soon called Stanley Livingstone and Me and Her. It's some of my footage and a lot of found footage Victoria Falls over a 30-year period. It's about colonialism and tourism. The next thing I'm moving into is how strange I think tourism is.

Do you see your work as a response to colonialism? Are you attempting to decolonize viewership?
I think a lot of my initial thoughts with this was being influence by a couple of things.

Several years ago, I started Super 8 and 8mm home movies from South Africa. As I was watching hundreds of hours it struck me. I realized if there's ever a black person on the screen, it's usually a panning shot, or some kind of a tilt. And it's the white family vacation, and they get in the shot, and then the camera cuts off quickly. And I just kept

thinking about, "Wow. I have hundreds of hours of footage of southern Africa, and I have no images of black people."

I think right around the time that really got into my head, I started revisiting lots of Jonas Mekas films. And I started thinking maybe I can, in a minor way, fill in this gap of representation of black, southern African people, on this Super 8 format. Zimbabwe never had over 1% white people or something like that. South Africa right now has 48 million people, and there's less than a million white people. But yet on my hours and hours of footage and you would think you're in Europe. There's rarely any black people in the footage. That's where I got really the initial idea, was I would like to fill in this gap of this record. And let's see African home movies.

What are some important films would you recommend for anyone looking to get into this style of documentary filmmaking? What inspires you?
When I was younger and getting really into documentary filmmaking, I watched Salesman (1969) for the first time and my head exploded. I just remember I kept pausing it. It probably took me seven hours to watch it. I really like Ephraim Asili. His stuff is really cool. And Akosua Adoma Owusu and Kevin Jerome Everson. I really gravitate towards films where there's a fracture between the visuals and the audio, but somehow they come together beautifully. I love it.

What do you want your audience to walk away with after watching Scenes from a Transient Home?
I want it to feel intimate, because it is. It's inside these people's homes. When we're at Masi's house, we're only in her little area, and at her sister's house. When we go to Kadoma, we're mainly around the house with the kids. I want people to feel that intimacy and that connection. I do play with the nostalgia a bit, and I want it to feel nostalgic like home movies. But also it goes back to just trying to find not only people that are underrepresented, but ideas. To see this woman, who's been separated from her children for 15 years go back home, I think it's important to show.

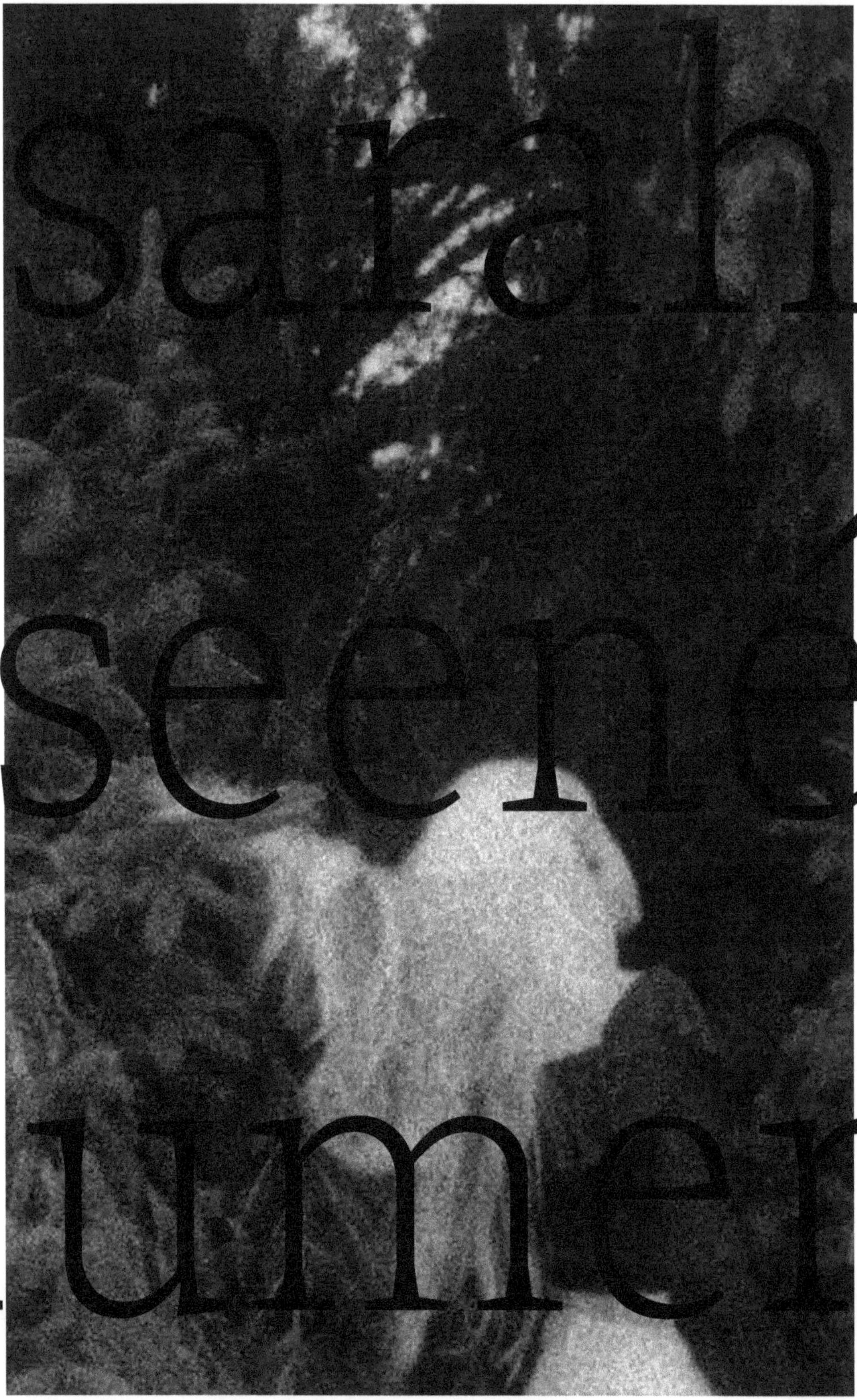
sarah

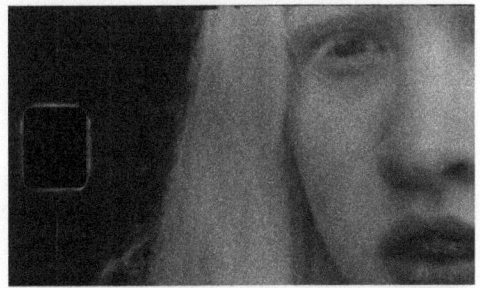

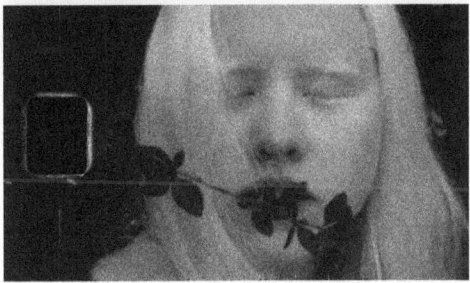

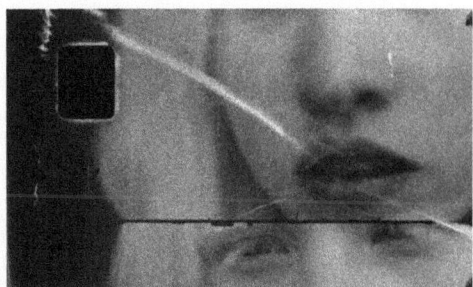

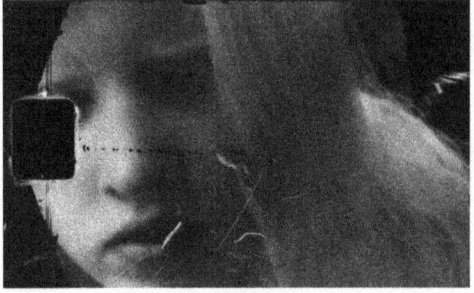

"Lumen"(meaning "light" in Latin) is a sensory film shot on Super-8 that portrays a young girl with oculocutaneous albinism. Despite the hypersensitivity caused by this genetic disease, the depigmentation of her skin and eyes gives her an extraordinary aura.

Why was it important to tell this story on film?
It was important to me to tell the story of Marlene , a 15-year-old girl suffering from oculocutaneous albinism. I choose to use Super-8 film because it summons the intimate and the sensory. It's precisely through these two prisms that I wanted to film her. The irregularities of the film, perforations, jump cuts and scratches caused by handprocessing are also part of this sensitive and hazardous creative process which contributes to a form of vibration and melancholy of the image. Black and white seemed obvious to me because it highlights the contrasts between the pale tone of her hair and her skin which give to Marlène the appearance of a negative film. Her body, like film emulsion, is by definition photosensitive.

What film stock did you use?
The film I used is Kodak Tri-x 200 iso. After handprocessing, I was able to see Marlene as positive on the negative film.

The film textures are beautiful. How did you process this film?
It's been done with a very DIY chaotic handprocessing technique. The mentor that showed me how to do it is the great filmmaker (and also my lover) Guillaume Vallée.

What do you hope your audience walks away with after watching this film?
I hope this short experimental documentary will shed some light, an awareness of what goes through people with albinism whom most of the time also suffers from severe visual impairments which worsen over the years. This filmed portrait of Marlène is a poetic allegory which aims to reveal a tangible reality.

Who are some of your artistic inspirations?

I am above all inspired by music. Some singers and groups who have a unique musical universe reinforced by a marked visual universe like Cocorosie, Agnes Obel, Émilie Simon. But since my main medium is analog photography, I am also very inspired by certain photographers such as Joel-Peter Witkin, Sarah Moon, Jane-Evelyn Atwood, Mary-Elen Mark, Roger Ballen or Dorothy Shoes. Also, some filmmakers are great sources of inspiration, like Lars von Trier (about whom I did my master's thesis in Cinema a few years ago) but also Harmony Korine (Gummo and Julien-donkey boy are my bibles) and Marie Losier, a French filmmaker who is making crazy and beautiful documentaries on 16mm. All of the artists mentioned here have in common the treatment of delicate subjects, of being attached to the human being and having disturbing universes.

What's next?

I just finished a new experimental self-portrait about my permanent tinnitus. It was created on Super-8 and handpainted. It's called Disappearing silence.

Do you have a favorite camera or tool when creating works on celluloid?

I started my artistic work with the Polaroid Sx70. It's one of my favourite cameras even though I use it a lot less than before. He's like an old friend whom I know very well, who is part of my daily environment. One of the cameras I use a lot is the Pentax K1000, it's my favourite. I also love my Super-8 Minolta XL 440 camera. I found in a garage sale when I was still living in the east of France in 2005. I didn't know at the time what I was going to do with it. Since the seller told me that it was working fine, I knew it would be useful to me one day. In addition, this camera is very beautiful, quite large and impressive, I keep it as a precious and magical object. She has always followed me in all my moves and it's finally 12 years later living in Canada that I used it to make my first Super-8 film.

Anything else to add?

For my film Lumen, it seemed interesting to me to work on the duality between the visible and the invisible, in order to evoke the visual impairment of the young girl at the core of the film. Going against what one might think is paradoxical at first glance is my way of conceiving visual art, as long as the process is full of delicacy. There are several types of visual impairment. Marlène's one allows her to perceive certain elements; her perception of shadows, lights, volumes and movements remains altered.

The shooting took place during summer, there was a lot of sun, we had to avoid direct light to avoid risking a deterioration of her vision but even in the shade of the trees, she had to close her eyes as the sun was aggressive. Her closed eyelids during the shoot added to the dreaminess of the film's poetry. The evanescence of the face and silhouette of this incredibly luminous young girl led me to find the film's title: Lumen which means "light" in Latin.

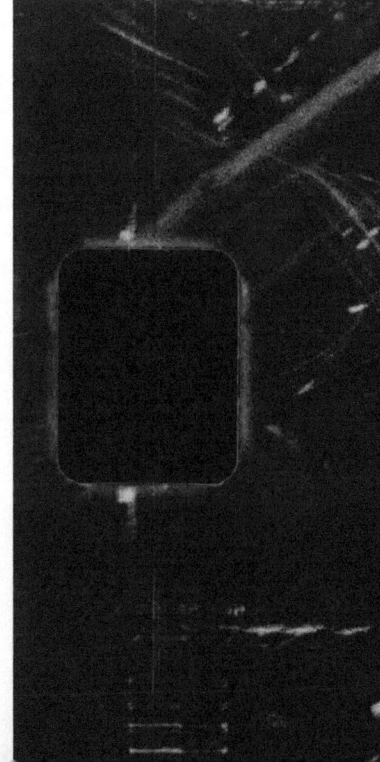

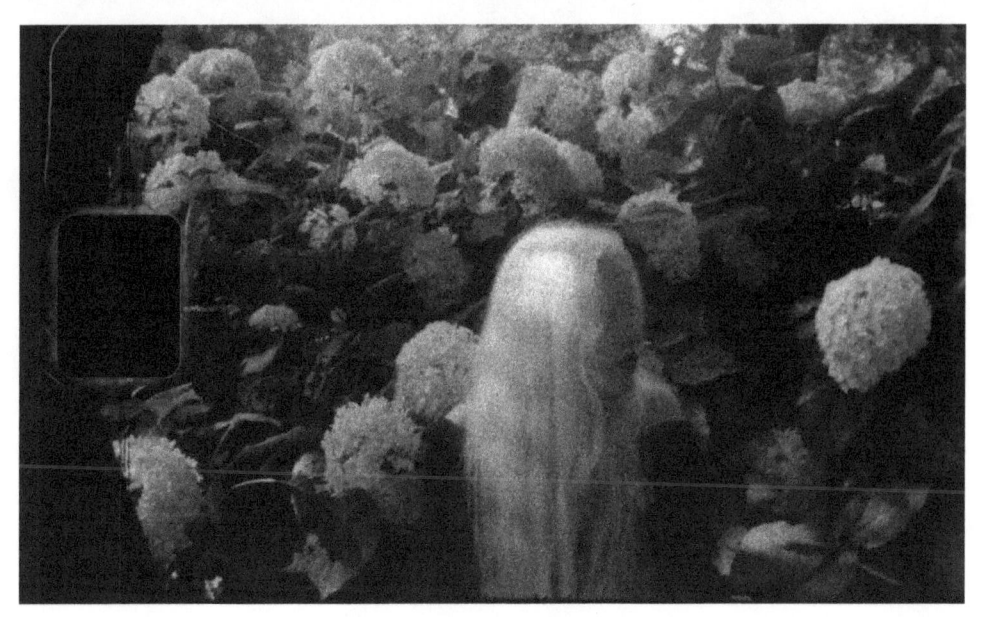

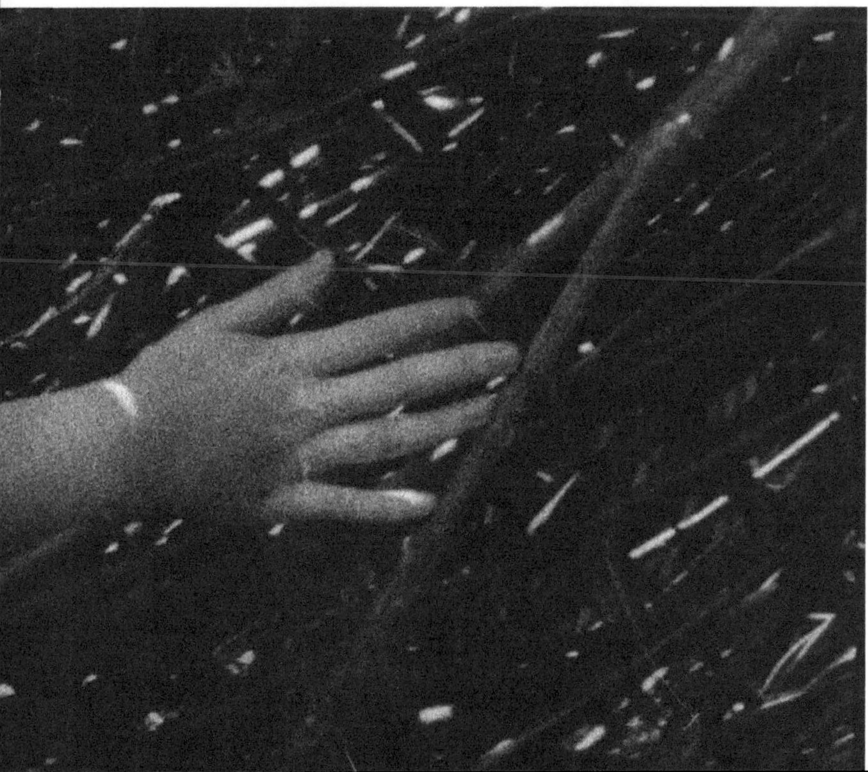

Guillaume Vallée

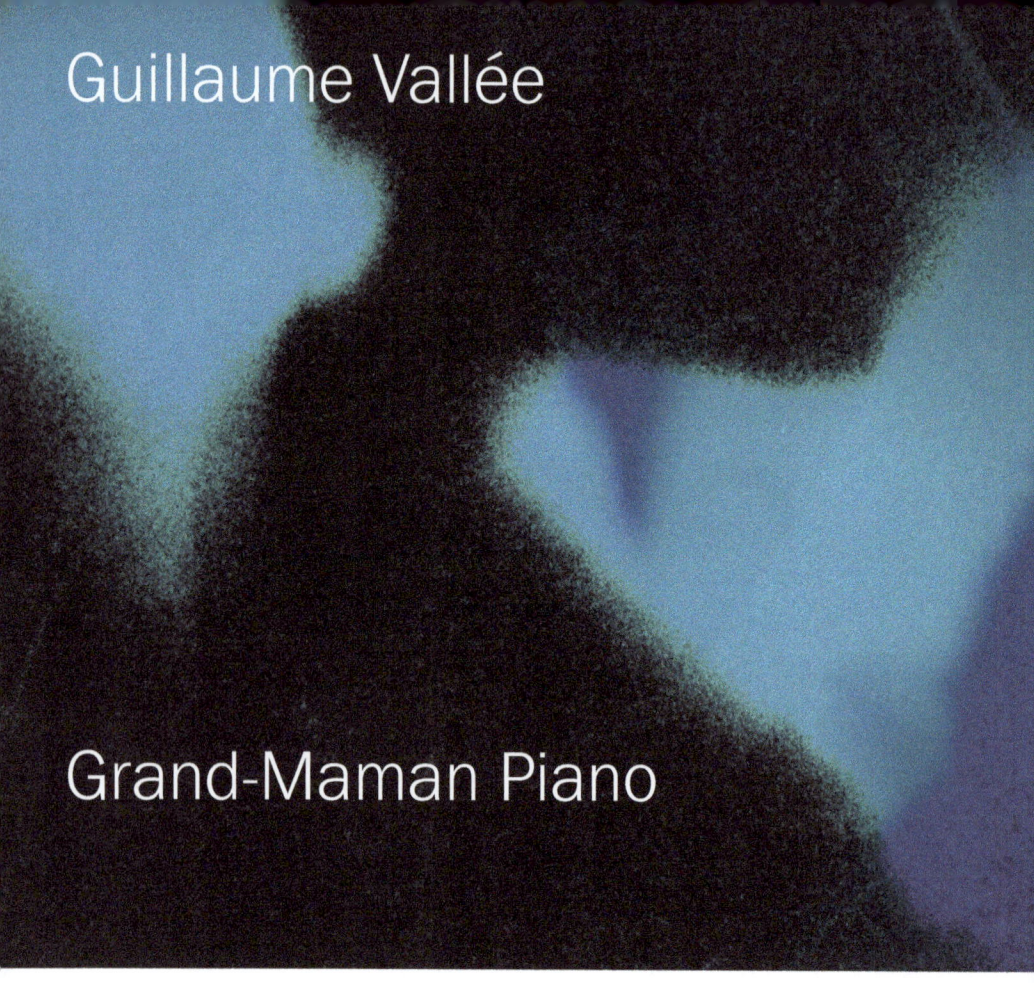

Grand-Maman Piano

TELL US ABOUT YOUR PROCESS WHEN CREATING GRAND-MAMAN PIANO

It all started when my mother left me a voicemail, using my grandmother's cell phone, to tell me she has passed away. I found that very weird to have this moment recorded, which is quite rare. It triggered the idea of making a film about her. I wanted to capture 3 different events in order to construct the narrative structure of the work. I used the last video moment of her, when she came for the first time to my place for my son William's birthday. It's been captured by my partner and wonderful artist, Sarah Seené, with her cell phone. I transferred the video as jpeg images (around 1100) and printed them, in black and white. I scanned all of them using colour filters to create a subtle flicker effect and I crumbled every piece of paper before scanning, as some sort of a goodbye ritual. For the second part, I wanted to have a physical trace of her while lying in the coffin. I brought my panoramic Vision-16 35mm camera to take photos at the funeral home. I found it interesting to document this moment, which is really intimate and full of sorrow, but for my project, I needed a distance to filter all of this. The 35mm hand-processed negative was the bridge to the moving images so I filmed the stills on Super8. The last part was during her ashes burial, shot on Super8 and hand-processed. Three parts before nothingness.

What film stocks did you use in creating these visuals?
Super8 Kodak Tri-X (7266)

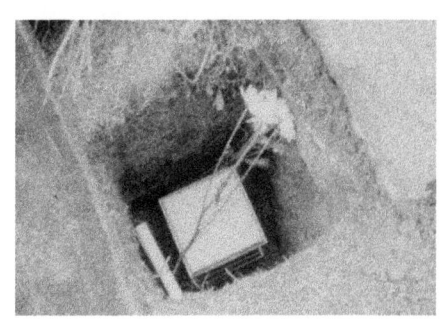

You use intimate moments throughout the film—footage of your grandmother in her final moments, her funeral. How do you approach depicting intimate moments on film?
I usually work with found footage and video signals, so when it comes to film actual people and moments, it's very refreshing. I also took the opportunity to reveal a little bit of myself and work with personal elements of my life. In that case, the loss of a beloved family member. Working in that way allows me to mourn through my creative process. Working with analog media allows me to be in touch with the film material and creates an intimate relation with it. By hand-processing and chemical intervention, I desacralized the image and gave back it's authentic imperfection. It's a moment in time and space, like everything else, and nothingness is inevitable.

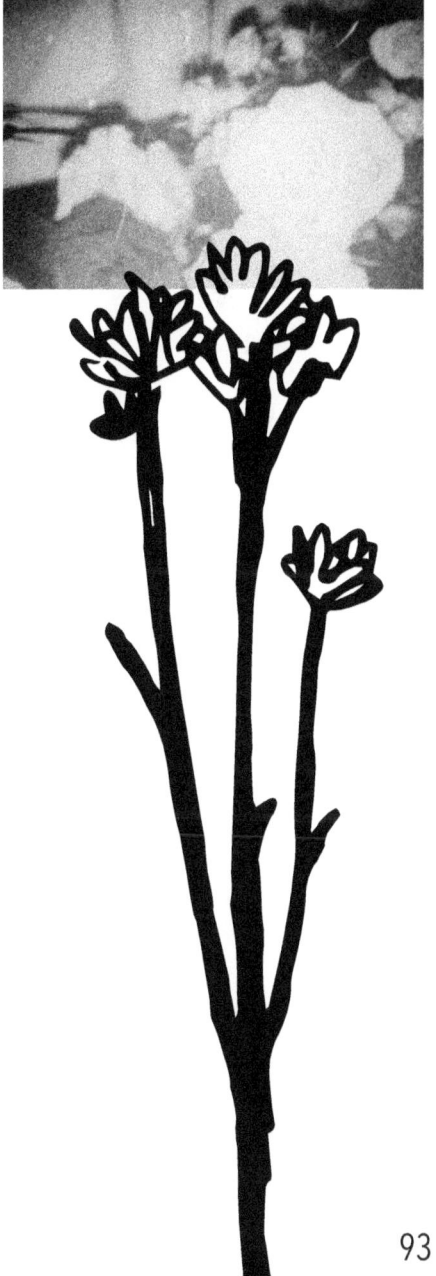

Would you consider this film an homage to your grandmother?
Yes, it's a bit of a homage.

What do you hope your audience walks away feeling after seeing this piece?
Touched and troubled.

What's next for you artistically?
I'm currently working on a new short film called "Monsieur Jean-Claude", a short 16mm experimental flick on toxic masculinity and stereotype in 80s-90s action movies using Jean-Claude Van Damme's roundhouse kick as the only source material. The footage comes from a 35mm trailer print of "The Quest", a feature film directed and interpreted by JCVD. This film is being created at Main Film (Montreal, CA) as part of their Film Factory residency program. So it's been and still is a lot of optical printing, contact printing, hand-processing and chemical interventions. I'm happy to be working again with my collaborator, Hazy Montagne Mystique, experimental musician based in Montreal, for the soundtrack. Will be done by the end of this year (hopefully).

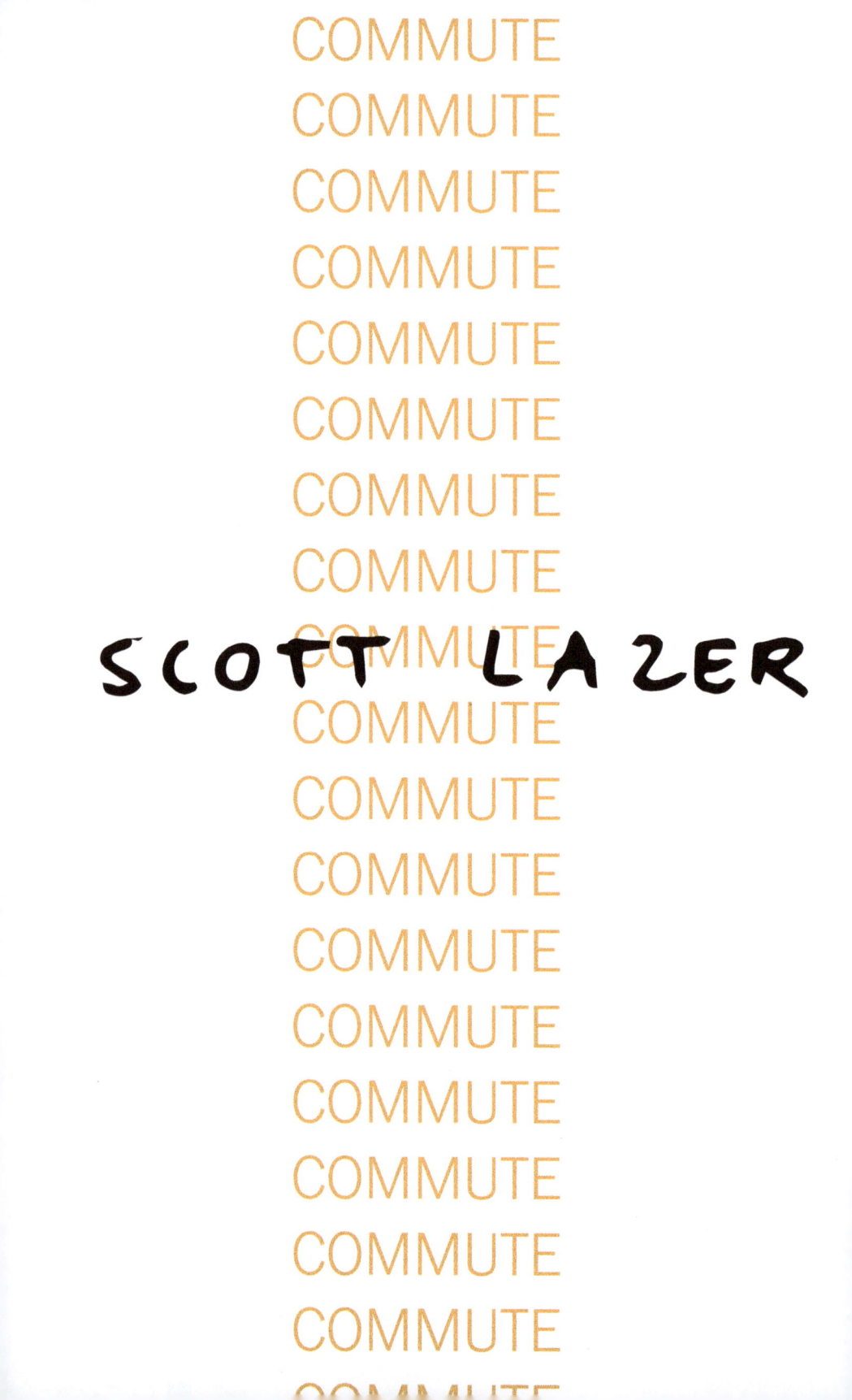

COMMUTE
COMMUTE
COMMUTE
COMMUTE
COMMUTE
COMMUTE
COMMUTE
COMMUTE
COMMUTE
COMMUTE
COMMUTE
COMMUTE
COMMUTE
COMMUTE
COMMUTE
COMMUTE
COMMUTE
COMMUTE

SCOTT LAZER

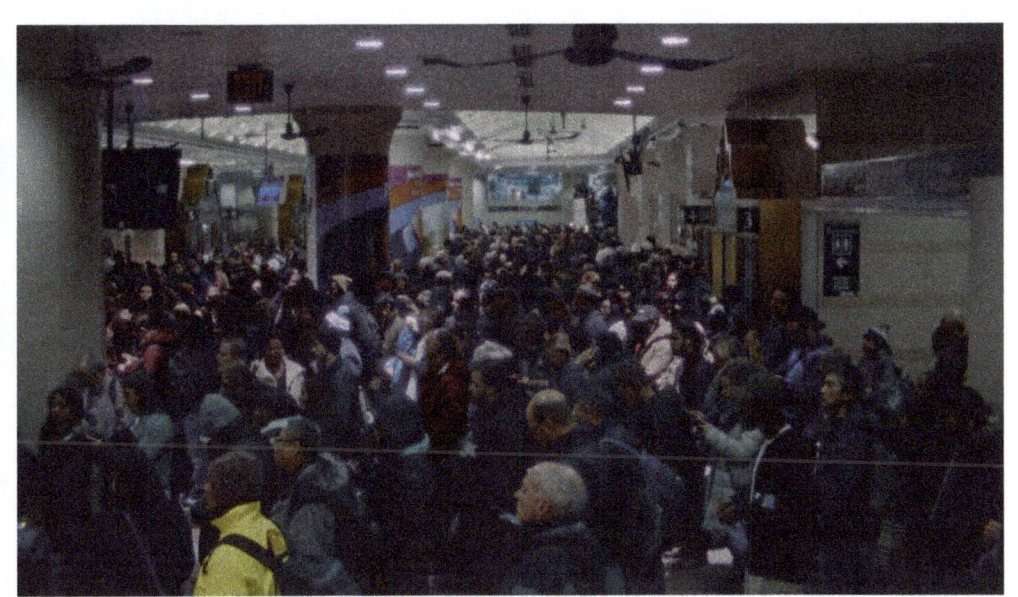

Why did you decide to shoot this project on film?

I'm a sucker for any movie or TV show set in New York - even the bad ones. I grew up in the South and only visited New York a couple times growing up, so cinema was what romanticized the city to me. When I had the idea to make Commute, I wanted to emulate some of the gritty streetscapes from movies I grew up on in the 90s. For both grain and cost, I decided on 16mm.

What film stock and camera did you use?

We shot this on Kodak 500T Color Negative film with an ARRI 416 camera.

Did you always know you wanted to shoot at Penn Station specifically? How did you get access/permission to shoot there?

The idea was inspired when I was a student at Rutgers University in New Jersey where I would take the train into the city and back. Again, having grown up in the South, my experience with trains was limited, so the first time I joined the platform stampede at Penn was extraordinary and overwhelming. That rush was what I wanted to capture in the film, and it had to be shot at Penn because that's where I experienced it.

We never got official permission to film there, but it was just cinematographer Lucas Millard and me, so we kept a small footprint and ducked the cops as much as we could. They hassled us a couple times, but we kept moving around until we shot through our rolls.

The quick edits in this piece really stand out and add to the overall frenetic feeling of trying to catch a train. Can you talk about your process here?

Even though this is a short piece, I wanted it to feel super dynamic with builds, peaks, and drops, and that tempo is entirely dictated by the music and the cut. It took me a while to find the edit, and I ended up going back to Penn two more times over two years to film more (the Friday afternoon before Christmas 2017, 2018, and 2019). The last thing I added was Wilson's voiceover, and once I got his timing right, it felt complete.

What do you want your audience to walk away feeling from this piece?

The word a lot of people have used when describing

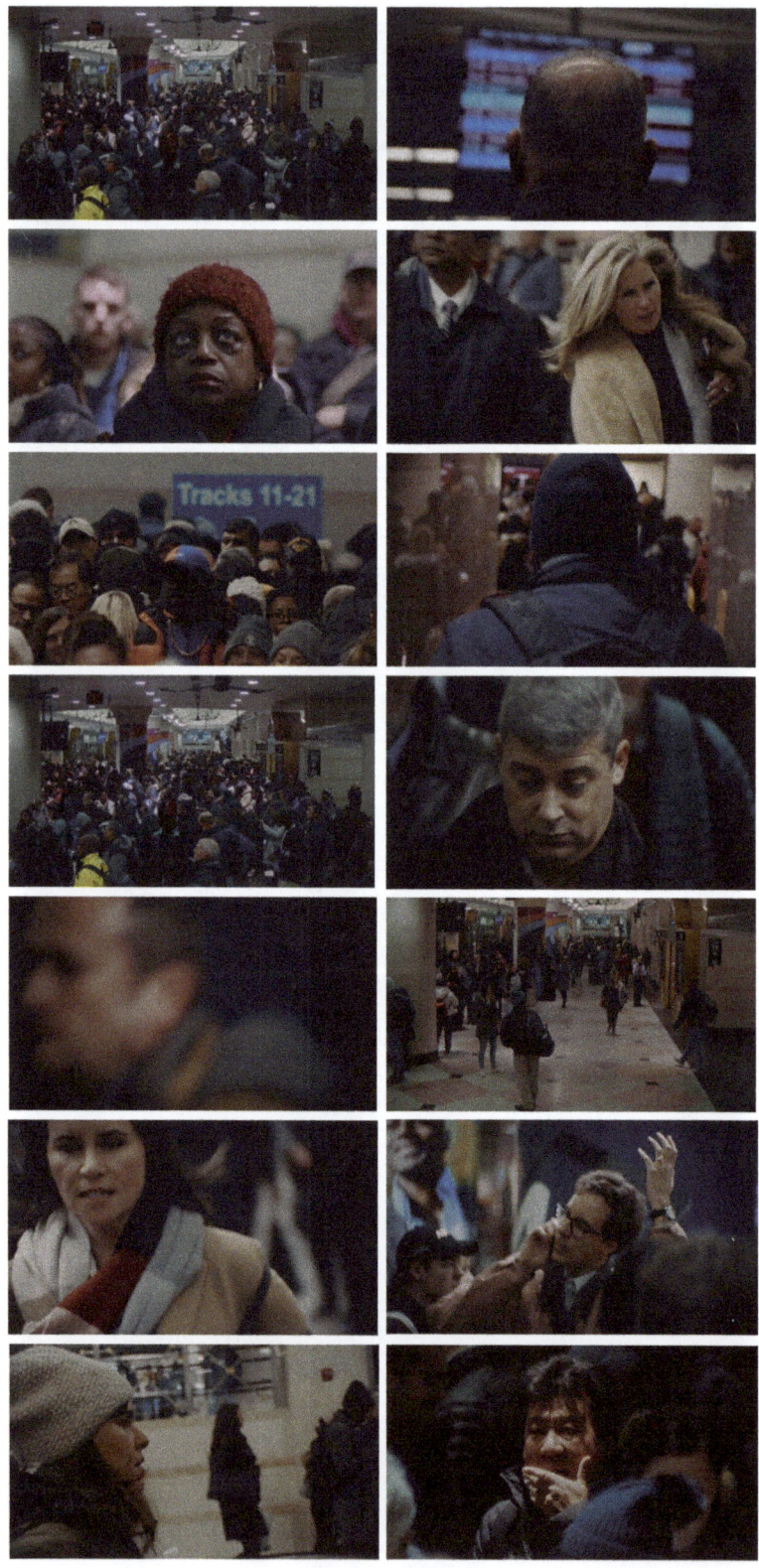

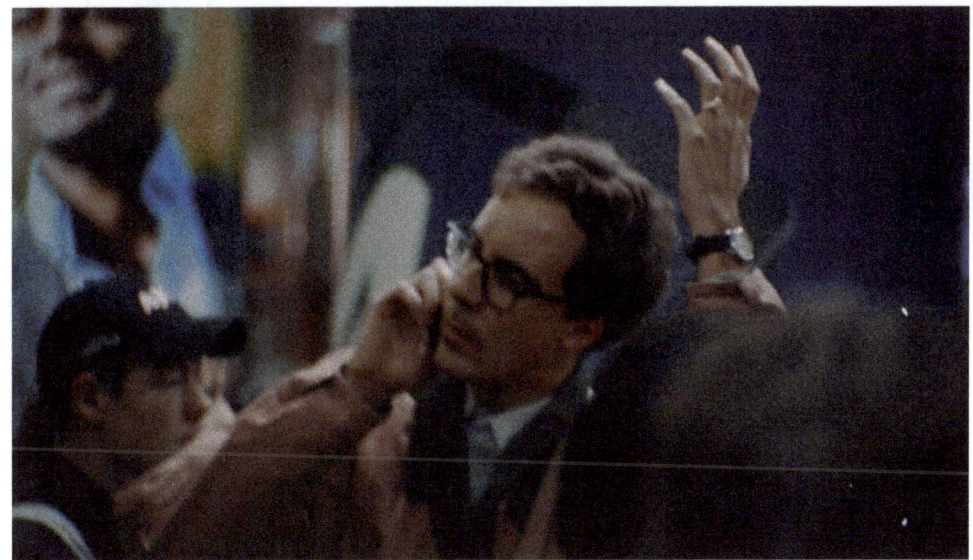

this film is "anxiety" which obviously makes sense. But in addition to that, I wanted to explore the out-of-body sensation you have sprinting after your train - that moment "you go away" as Wilson puts it and become one with your fellow commuters. It's like riding a wave as it crashes, when the ocean takes full control of your body, which feels both terrifying and sublime.

How did it feel to get a Vimeo Staff pick?

A lot of the work I've done has been in the music space, so I'm always standing next to other artists helping them with what is ultimately their projects and their broader visions. Films I make in that capacity don't entirely feel like mine. But Commute was different. It was personal, it belongs to me, and that it has resonated with people and caught the attention of institions like the Vimeo staff has been especially gratifying because it was just something I wanted to make.

What advice would you give other filmmakers wanting to shoot on film?

This was the first project I shot entirely on film, so I don't have much experience shooting analog. If you're like me, I highly recommend finding a collaborator with a lot of celluloid experience because it can be unforgiving.

Any new film projects you want to share?

I'm releasing my next film, Visitors, at the end of September. It's a short documentary that was filmed at the Storm Area 51 event in the Nevada desert last year. It's played at a few film festivals this year, so I'm making it available on my Vimeo channel just like I did with Commute. I have a few other projects all at different stages that I'm working on as well.

Anything else you want to share about yourself and your process?

This has obviously been a difficult year for everyone to say the least. And while it's challenged me to examine myself and what I want to do with my work, I'm actually more inspired than ever to tell stories I'm passionate about. This will be a turning point for a lot of artists.

Tom Schulte

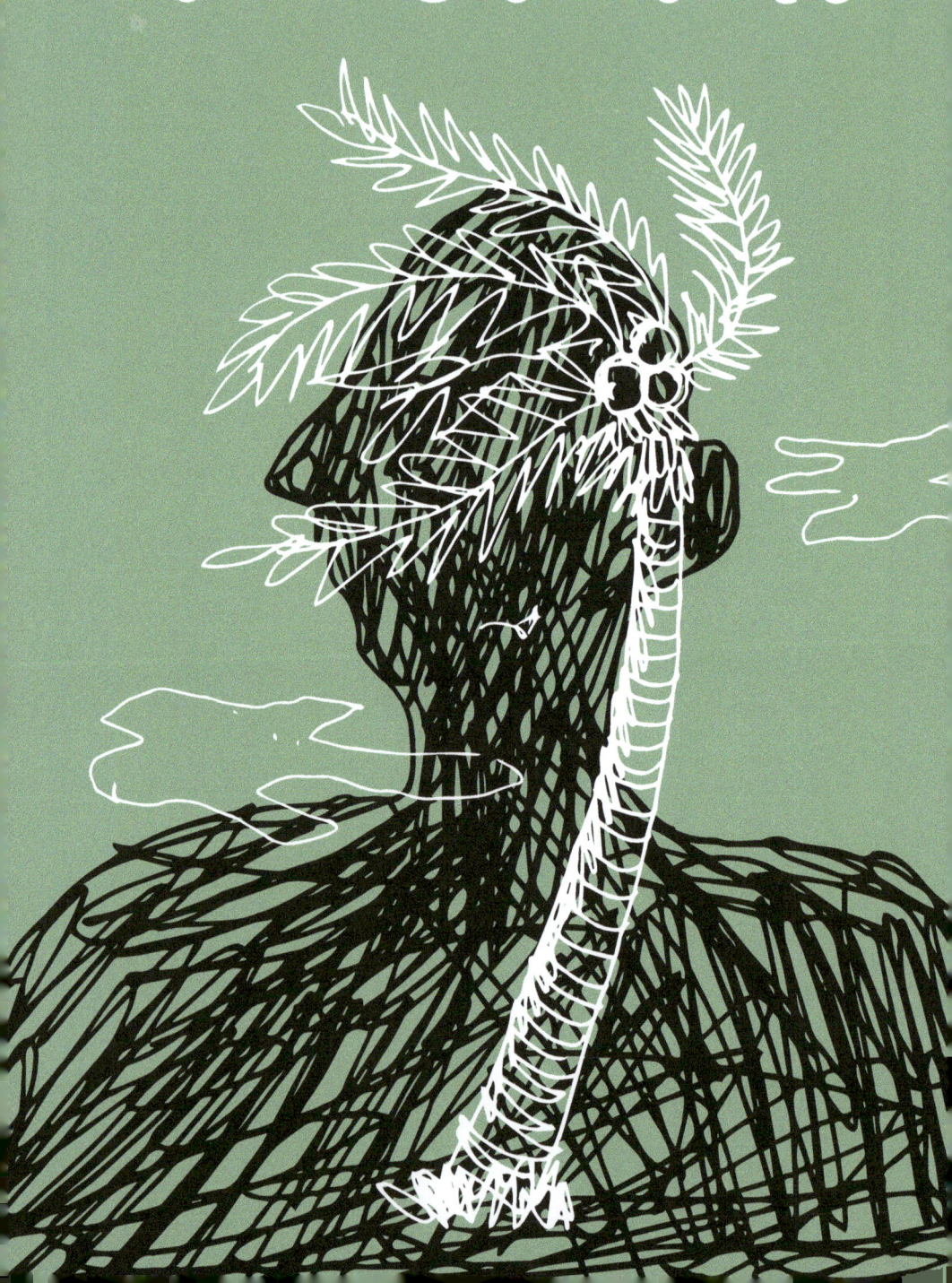

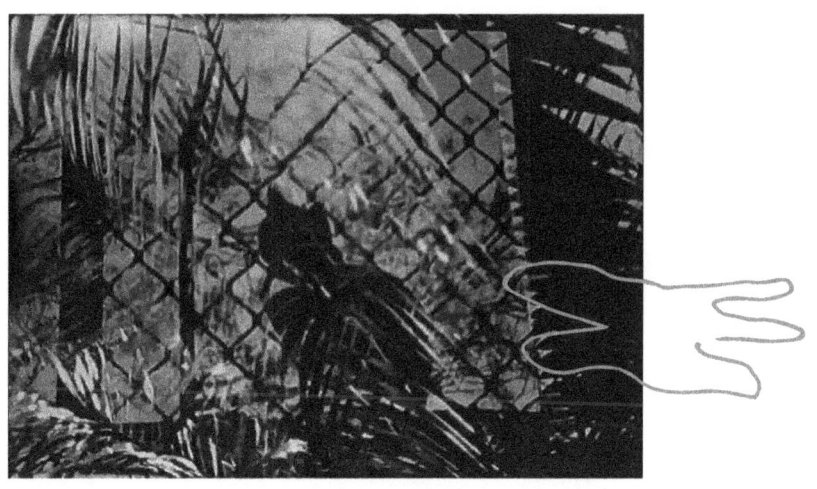

If you've ventured into the curious world of film, chances are you've seen a photo somewhere that was exposed twice (or more). It can be a smashing effect, and really it's not that hard to multi-expose with still photography, especially on 35mm considering that many new and old cameras have the ability to do so, or with the simple act in rewinding and using the same film canister again (and again, and again... if you wish).

But how about motion picture film?

For this particular info/guide on exposing movie film multiple times, I chose Super 8mm because this format is probably the most accessible, and used frequently by many from amateurs to professionals. It certainly was my first step into motion picture film, and we can all agree that general interest in Super 8mm has blown up in recent years. In turn there is no doubt that some film-users would like to multi-expose 8mm film. So for my fellow Super 8mm users, here I shall give you 3 options:

If you want to multi expose the nice n easy way, you could either: 1. get a camera (Nizo801M, Agfa Movexoom, Canon 1014XLS etc - they all tend to be in the higher grade) that has the ability to rewind film (e.g for lap dissolves), or 2. get a backwinder from eBay or your local classifieds. Done, you can now rewind and multi-expose some film. BUT here might arise a problem for you: only 90cm (3ft) or so of film can be rewound at any one time due simply to how the film cartridges are made. There is a risk of jamming the film, or breaking the cartridge if the film is rewound any further. It is also best to avoid repeated rewinds for the same reasons.

And so here is option 3: For anyone wishing to multi-expose an entire cartridge of Super 8mm film, get one of these fine things: a Kaccema Reloadable Cartridge.

They're often available on eBay for 10-20USD a pop, and as you can see they look just like a standard super 8 cartridge, but the Kaccema cartridges can be opened to it's core for reloading an entire 15m (50ft) of film.

Simply put, you must extract all 15m (50ft) of film out of the cartridge you used (e.g. Kodak Kodachrome), then move it across to the Kaccema cartridge so the film is ready to be exposed again. As with many processes involving film, this film-extraction to reloading must be done in total darkness.

THINGS YOU'LL NEED:

- Super 8mm film that you've shot
- Kaccema Reloadable Cartridge
- A ring of some sort
  (approx 22mm diameter, 8mm thick)
- Sticky Tape
- Scissors
- Practise and Patience

THE CARTRIDGE COMES IN 4 MAIN PARTS:

1. Front cover
2. Film-loading and film-takeup chambers
(largest part)
3. Film take-up wheel/cog
4. Back cover

The covers serve no purpose other than to cover and light seal the main inner part (film loading and takeup areas. I will refer to this inner large part as the cartridge in method below. There is also the pressure plate mechanism which can be left alone if positioned correctly.

There's no easy way to do it, there's no doubt it's tricky to do, but if you want to give it a go, check out the images and accompanying text below as a guide.

NOTES:

Use some film that's already been developed to practise in daylight

Search up 'Kaccema cartridges' on the internet. There are some videos available to walk you through the process

You can make your own reloadable cartridges with careful disassembly of kodak/agfa/fuji cartridges (search the web)

Tip for double exposing: Shoot contrast-y scenes on your first footage of film, for any footage shot on the reloaded cartridge will show better on the underexposed (dark) areas of your initial footage. You might find more pleasing results if you meter for highlights.

DIRECTIONS

1 - Take yourself, your film and all the tools you'll need and go into a dark-room.

2 - Lay out your cartridges and tool in front of you. Remember where everything is.

3 - Disassemble Kaccema cartridge and carefully layout in front of you. Remember exactly where everything is.

4 - Extract the film you've shot out of your cartridge and roll it anti-clockwise around your ring. *Hold the leader at the top of the roll, with the leader sticking out towards the right hand side. Emulsions side out, sprockets up (towards you).

5 - Place the roll of film on the film-loading side of the cartridge. Carefully thread the leader above and past the two rollers on the upper left and right hand side of the cartridge.

6 - Whilst holding the roll of film in place, pull the leader on top of the pressure plate, then insert into the 'slit' just below the plate.

7 - Flip the cartridge. Pull and guide the film through the lowermost 'passage', then around the rounded corner.

8 - Pick up the film takeup wheel/cog. You will notice that when it's inserted into the cartridge it will only turn clock-wise.Therefore, once you've threaded the film around the rounded corner, cut off a bit of sticky tape, then attach the leader on the wheel itself.

9 - Rotate the wheel a couple times with your fingers to make sure it's attached correctly. And make sure the film is placed and threaded correctly.

10 - Maintain the tension of the film and put the covers on. You may need to hold the film in place so it doesn't slip out of anywhere.

11 - Shoot your second-exposure.

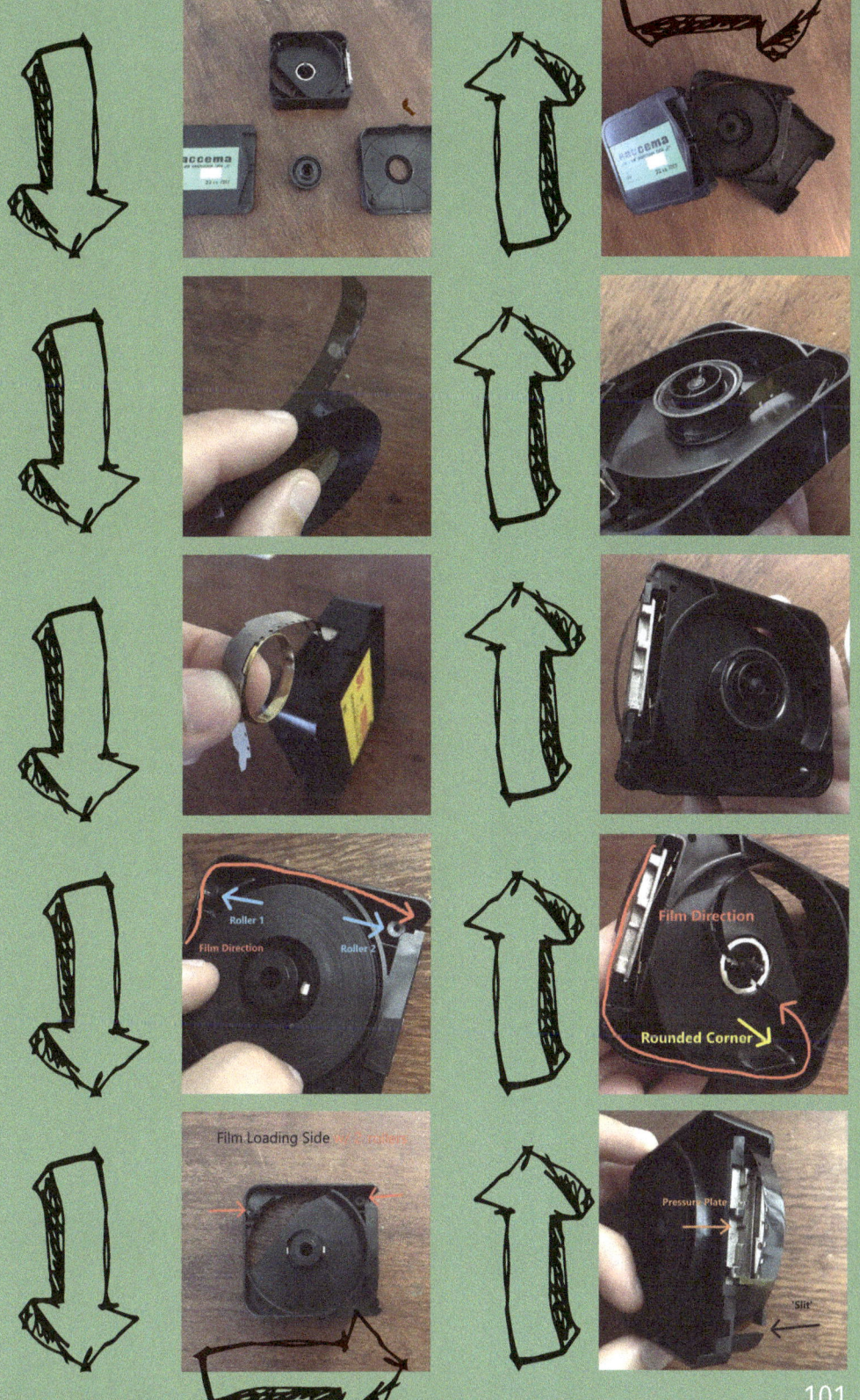

ZOE GRACE MARQUEDANT

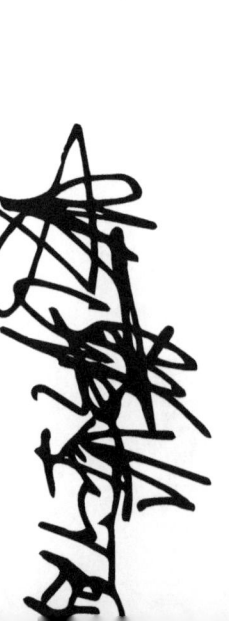

Studying Degradation in Disaster

Instead of the news, I read definitions of Vinegar Syndrome and thought about the inevitabilities of conservation. About the almost ephemeral quality of time-based media. About nitrate and opening day quality. The unstoppable final stages of deterioration. The lack of funding, lack of low-light environments, breathable enclosures. The infectious nature of acidic vapors.

There is an acquaintance with brittleness when it comes to books, maps, telegrams, paper. Yellowed pages. Movie posters. Museum exhibit items shown in glass cases with clock-like humidity trackers. The passage of time is present in libraries, the stagnant smell of the stacks. Is it dust? Or unmoving air and an ancient unvacuumed carpet. The fragility is familiar. An edition of Dickens gives way to mites, loose binding, sunlight, and no one is surprised. The senses are intuned to this reality. This smell of damp.

But how does an image fade? Plastics, emulsions, chemicals all sound permanent. They are man-made things, harsh to breathe in and firm to the touch. How can time have any effect on them? Are they not the infallible medium? Acetate sound too scientific to be so ultimately weak. Between studio executives, chemists, art students, mad scientists did no one think of this?

The Image Permanence Institute sounds like something out of SciFi. A snapshot is a capturing. Film an event made solid, made light. Rewind buttons, second screenings, matinees, double-headers, summer blockbusters, reasons to rewatch favorites. A film strip is not single-use. And so how does it not last, not withstand. How is it not forever? When does it's proverbial spine crack?

There are evident errors. Moments to blame tools, acknowledge mistakes, human nature. Scratches and particles. Frictions. Wear and tear. The evidence of poor development, the remanents of chemicals, of unsealed or unsafe conditions. Basements. Rusted boxes in the Czech Republic. Hot rooms. Fingertips. Paths to decay. Without them, how does the inevitable creep in? When does it become futile?

There is the unavoidable truth of acid. Of catalyst, acceleration, consumption. Vinegar Syndrome. The smell of a reaction taking place. The possibility of degradation. The actions of acetic acid becoming both household and industrial. The word "vinegar" having been derived from the Latin, "vinum" meaning wine and "acer" meaning sour. Acidic. Harmful, but how can you blame what exists in oranges, pineapples, strawberries. Occurs organically. It's a mere reaction with water. An odor.

The irreversible business of edges and escape. Encircling. Reels. Canisters. Shrinking, curling, warping. Losing flexibility. The reaction autocatalytic, feeding on itself. Speeding up. Unable to be stopped. An eyeful of an apocalypse in a can. Is it preventable or certain? What of sieves and proper handling?

The causes of decay are so inherent, so predictable. The factors so casual. It is in film's nature to fall apart. To become embrittled. To buckle. Show visible channeling. Conditions can be perfected. Films kept passively. Cold, dry storages built. Temperature and airflow controlled. But this only moves the inevitable into the future. The process is extended to a hopeful hundreds of years. But what then.

How can life be extended? When anywhere there is moisture there is slow, continuous reaction. The search for vapors continues indefinitely and I question whether or not archival work is an act of alchemy. The minor miracles of preservation. To work in terms of weeks per scene. Carefully opening, unraveling. Winding through. Moving from medium to medium, from film stock to film stock, to a more stable format.

Working in ventilation. Working with unstable elements. Working at suggested fifteen-minute intervals. Wearing defusion tubes on pockets and lapels. Knowing how acid acts on faces, hands. All to reproduce sounds, clean the strips, scan, and digitalize. Frame by frame. For hundreds of thousands of frames per film. The migration of material between generations. To the next form of the moving image

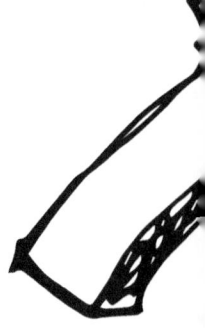

Racing against a form of disintegrating. Like refreezing an iceberg. Knowing the process is accelerating. Once onset. It shortens the life of the film. With the only hope being early diagnosis. Detection of a known stage of decay.

The archeology of restoration. The piecing together of negatives and prints. Remanents of technicolor masterpieces. Black and whites reduced to snippets. Surviving elements, as it looked through the camera, to retrace the foundation of the film, extracting and extrapolating pictures, navigating the ethics of artifacts and splice marks, cleaning up dark lines. The delicate process.. The deciphering of shadows. The intensions of colorists. Minning scenes for the thought processes of their creators. Taking care not to overcorrect, influence, actually change the intension of the film.

All to preserve the feeling of seeing something, as it was meant to be. As if you were the first person to watch it. Trying to maintain that shimmer of the silver screen and the feeling of having to stumble back into the world after the last scene.

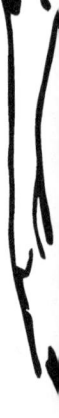

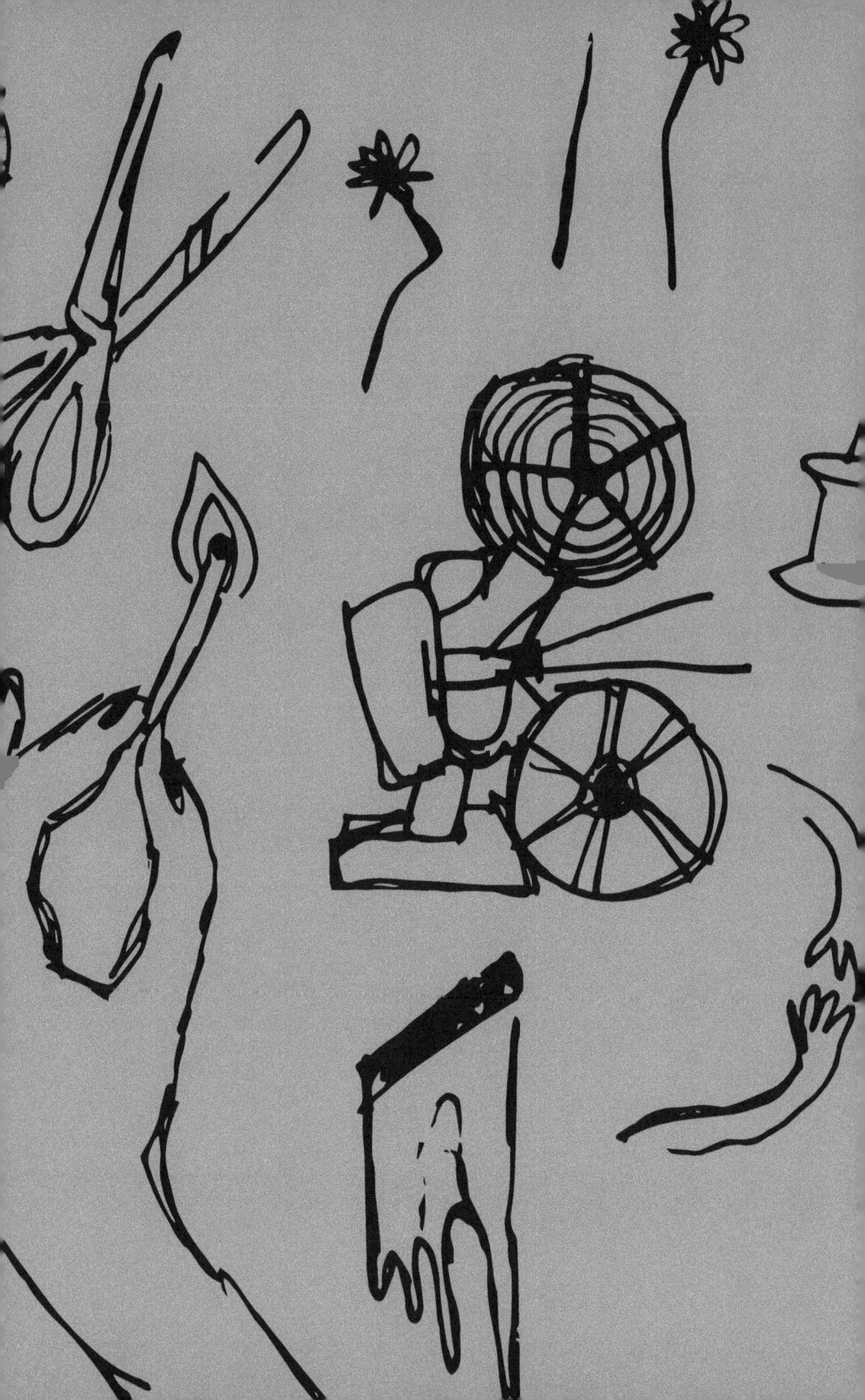

"My passion for analogue photography grew with me, when I was a little girl photography was only analogue."

Disposable cameras that we took on a school trip or on holiday at the sea were analog, so for me it was just going back to where I left off. The parenthesis of digital was more an experience that started and ended, because my way of seeing is with the grain and the colors of the film. Absolutely the film has a poetry that makes my heart beat.

I have no format preferences I use both the 35 mm and the 120 mm. By choice I prefer the 120 mm for the project called "URBAN ACTIONS OF PHOTOGRAPHY : VISUAL POETRY"

In the darkroom I prepare several contact prints, I cut little photographs with wavy scissors and the street will be their gallery, I will entrust them to her, her wooden doors, her windows, her peeling walls of buildings and the marble slabs of her streets.

My photographic message will be posted in the streets in an intrusive way, a philosophical message that can be adopted and brought home, or left where you will find it.

I use different kind of cameras: Nikon FM2, Canon AE1, Weltaflex, Pentax 645, Voigtländer Vito CLR , instant cameras and I love use toy cameras like Big Holga 120N or something similar like Photostar camera, one plastic camera absolutely unknown but results are amazing.
At the moment my favorite camera is Canon AE1

with Russian Zenit Helios 44-6 lens. I'm making a series of photographs taken with various analogue machines printed on the yellowed pages of old books and on vintage ephemera.

The idea of combinating photography and old books and old ephemera was born because I collect a large amount of old books and old ephemera and working with paper that smell of trees and wood is amazing.

I like the feeling of the past.

Reading is a great source of inspiration for me, it has always been. At the moment I am deeply inspired by the reading of Amalia Guglielminetti's poems and novels. She was an Italian poetess and writer of the early twentieth century. Amalia experienced several tragedies in her early years and her response was to write verse expressing her feelings.

I have always been influenced by silent films, experimental films and surrealist cinema that use irrational imagery and dream symbolism.

Impossible for me not remember Sergei Parajanov, soviet film director and artist of Armenian descent, he made some of the most beautiful films ever seen. His films were the reason of my trip in Armenia I did last year.

roxy beat

There are many artists, photographers, writers, film directors, courageous women, activists, who inspire me from various walks of my life. Especially I'm fascinated by women who makes art who help us to define our feelings and our role and they move away from voyeurism and sexual objectification of woman.

I'm proud to be one of them.

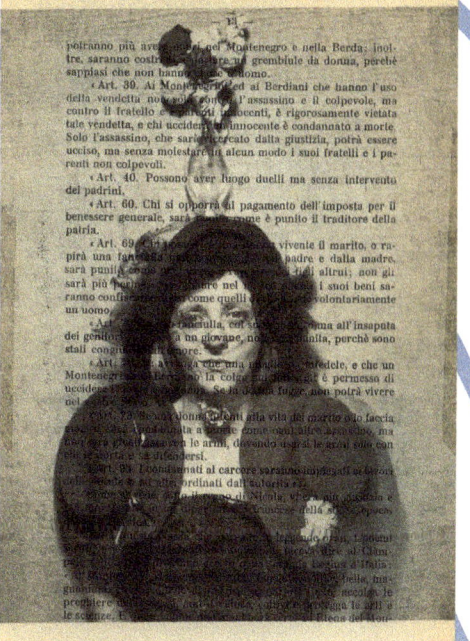

www.ingramcontent.com/pod-product-compliance
Lightning Source LLC
Chambersburg PA
CBHW040111180526
45172CB00010B/1306